BIOLOGY AND GEOLOGY
SECONDARY
BY ME

Francisco Márquez Álvarez

THE EVOLUTION OF LIFE

Contents

01 Cells: the basic units of life — 4
1. The composition of living things — 6
2. From microscopes to cell theory — 7
3. The organisation of living matter — 9
4. Prokaryotic cells — 11
5. Eukaryotic cells — 13
6. Components of eukaryotic cells — 15

Discovery techniques:
Observing plasmolysis in plant cells — 24
Observing cellular forms in infusions — 25

Read and think:
Stem cells: the secret to change — 28

02 Cell reproduction — 30
1. The reproduction of living things — 32
2. The cell cycle — 35
3. Chromosomes — 38
4. Cell division — 41
5. The sexual reproduction cycle — 43
6. Life cycles — 46

Discovery techniques:
Making a karyotype — 48
Observing mitosis in plant cells — 49

Read and think:
Margarita Salas: the success of a pioneer — 52

03 The inheritance of traits — 54
1. The birth of genetics — 56
2. Fundamental concepts of genetics — 57
3. Mendel's laws — 59
4. Exceptions to Mendel's laws — 63
5. The chromosomal theory of inheritance — 64
6. Interpretation of Mendel's laws — 65
7. Human genetics — 69

Discovery techniques:
Solving a test cross problem — 73

Read and think:
New technique to prevent certain inheritance diseases — 76

04 Molecular genetics — 78
1. Nucleic acids — 80
2. Functions of nucleic acids — 82
3. Mutations — 86
4. Genetic engineering — 88
5. Biotechnology and bioethics — 92

Discovery techniques:
Learn about the polymerase chain reaction — 94
Solve molecular genetics problems — 95

Read and think:
How the Jellyfish's green light revolutionised bioscience — 98

Glossary — 100
Big thinkers — 104

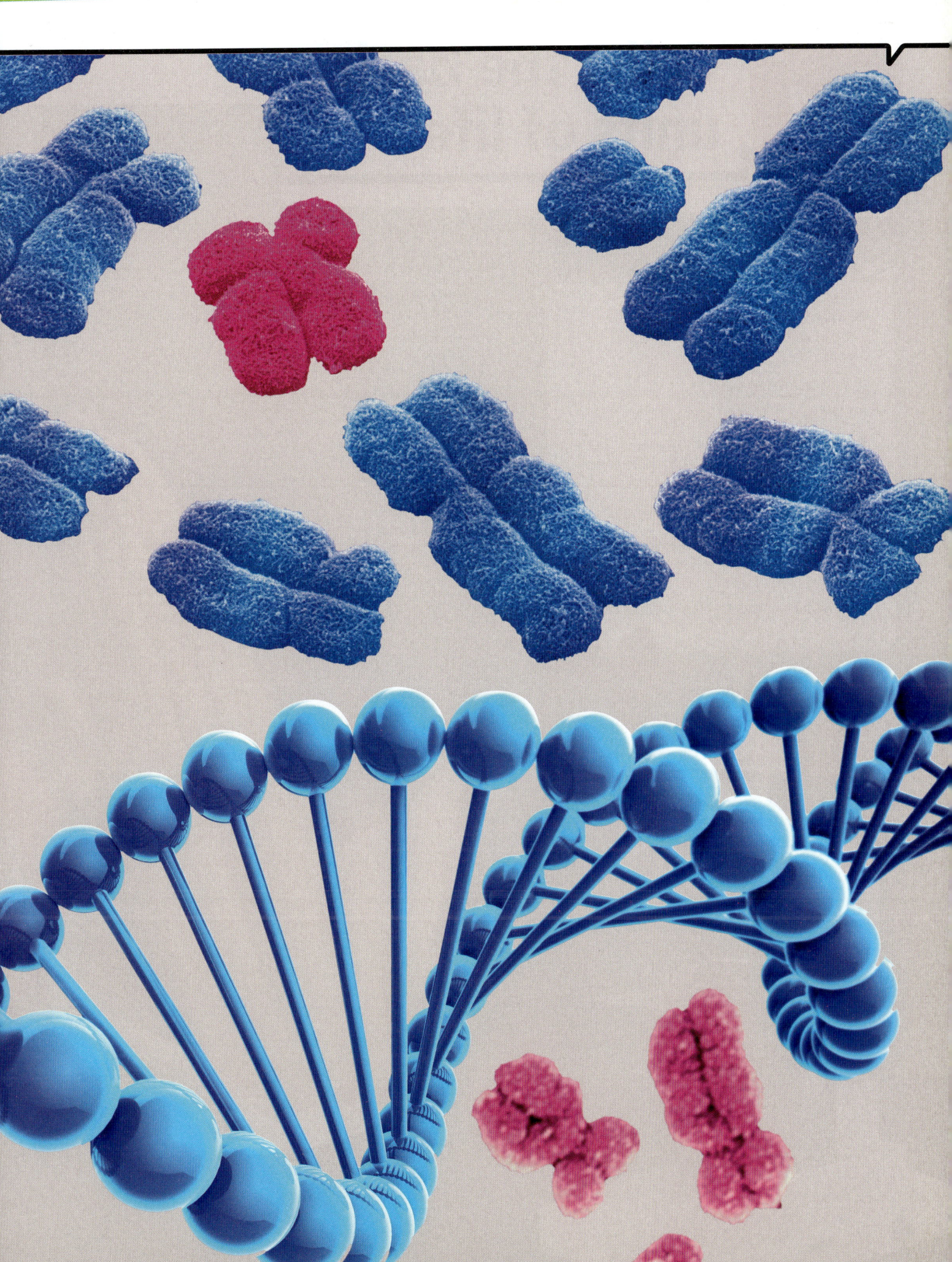

The evolution of life

01 Cells: the basic units of life

<<LOOKING BACK

- When was the microscope invented and by whom? Why was this discovery so important?
- Who discovered cells?
- Who coined the term 'cell' and why?
- Based on their complexity, what two types of cells are there? What are the differences between them?
- Which type of cell is shown in image B?
- Look at image A. Are maize plants unicellular or multicellular organisms? Explain why.
- What components are common to all cells?

Maize (*Zea mays*)

Microscopic cities

Once upon a time, there was a city protected by a strong wall, with ports of entry that controlled who and what could enter and exit. Inside, there was everything the city needed to flourish. There were blacksmith's shops where important materials were produced, windmills to transform the forces of nature into useful energy, farmer's fields where food was grown, and warehouses for storing goods and waste. Such things were distributed via a system of roads and wagons that circulated to collect waste and help fix things that needed to be repaired.

At the centre of the city was the castle. It had its own wall and all movement in or out went through guarded entrances. In the castle lived the queen, the city's most knowledgeable inhabitant. Her orders dictated everything that happened in the city. If the city grew too big, she even had the power to make it magically split into two identical copies … Magic or not?

- What do you think this text is really describing?
- What is the 'city wall' an analogy of? What about the 'castle wall'?
- What is the 'queen'? What does she control?
- What do you think the different aspects of the city are meant to represent?
- Instead of a medieval city, what other analogy could describe this subject?

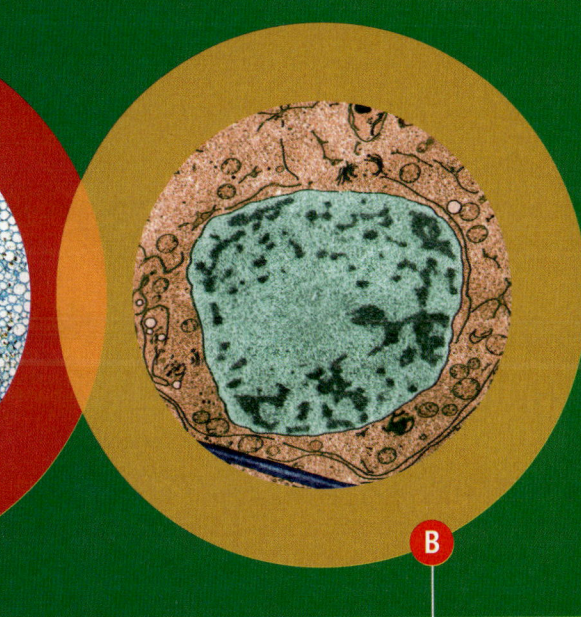

A Section through the root of a maize plant

B Cell of a maize root tip

- What macromolecules are found in living things?
- What does cell theory state?
- What does the endosymbiotic theory state?
- What are the differences between a nucleus and a nucleoid?
- Do plant cells have centrosomes?
- Where is cellular respiration performed?
- How can we observe the process of plasmolysis?
- How can we cultivate microorganisms?

UNIT 01 Cells: the basic units of life

1. The composition of living things

> What macromolecules are found in living things?

All living things share a chemical composition that differentiates them from inert things, such as rocks and air.

- **Inert things**, such as rocks, are formed of **inorganic chemical compounds**. These compounds include chemical elements found in plentiful supply on Earth: oxygen (O), silicon (Si), aluminium (Al), iron (Fe) and calcium (Ca).
- **Living things** are formed of inorganic and organic chemical compounds:

  – **Inorganic compounds**. The main inorganic compounds found in living things are **water** and **mineral salts**.

  – **Organic compounds**. These are **carbohydrates**, **lipids**, **proteins** and **nucleic acids**. They mainly comprise four chemical elements: carbon (C), hydrogen (H), oxygen (O) and nitrogen (N). The organic compounds of living things are very varied, complex and, in many cases of large molecular size, in which case, they are known as **macromolecules**.

> Most of the volume of living things is taken up by water, an inorganic component that can make up between 70% and 99% of the total.
>
> However, in spite of their lesser proportion, organic compounds are responsible for the structural characteristics and the activity of living things.

CARBOHYDRATES

○ These molecules, also called **sugars**, vary in size. The simplest are **monosaccharides**. The most complex are **polysaccharides**: many monosaccharides joined together. They provide energy and also have a structural function, as they form part of cell walls and the woody tissue of plants.

LIPIDS

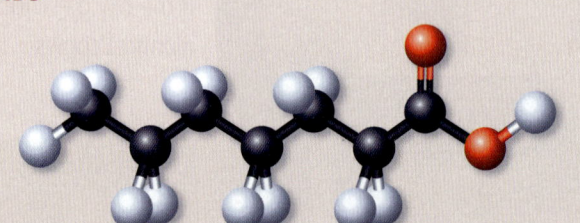

○ The main part of their structure is a carbon and hydrogen chain. They are insoluble in water and can perform functions related to structure (forming part of cell membranes), energy (as fuel reserves) or cell regulation (acting as chemical messengers).

PROTEINS

○ These are macromolecules formed by **amino acids** joining together. The combination of 20 different amino acids creates an endless number of different proteins. They have a regulatory function, controlling chemical reactions and transporting substances, and a structural function, given that they form part of skeletons, skin, nails and cell coverings.

NUCLEIC ACIDS

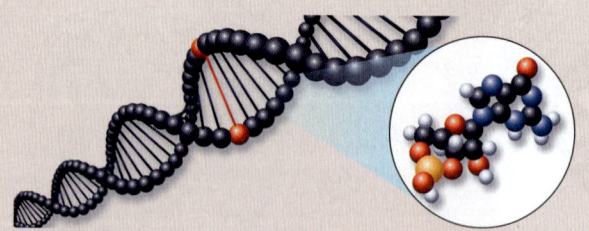

○ These are macromolecules formed by **nucleotides** joining together. The combination of four different nucleotides allows for a wide variety of different molecules. The main function of the nucleic acids is to hold hereditary information, which controls cell functioning, and pass it on to descendants.

ACTIVITIES

1. What are the most common chemical elements in living things? Can these elements also be found in non-living things?

2. Would it be correct to say that living things are made up more of inorganic substances than of organic substances? Explain your answer.

2. From microscopes to cell theory

> What does cell theory state?

The compound microscope first appeared at the end of the 16th century. Its invention is attributed to Dutch spectacle makers Hans and Zacharius Janssen and was subsequently developed by Galileo. This invention enabled the observations that culminated in the establishment of the **cell theory**.

In 1665, **Robert Hooke** (1637–1703) observed under a compound microscope that the plant material of cork was made up of numerous pores that reminded him of the cells of a honeycomb. In fact, it was Hooke who coined the term *cell*. What he observed in reality were not cells, but the frameworks formed by the cell walls remaining in place after cell death. It was then proven that cells were not empty, as different structures could be seen inside of them.

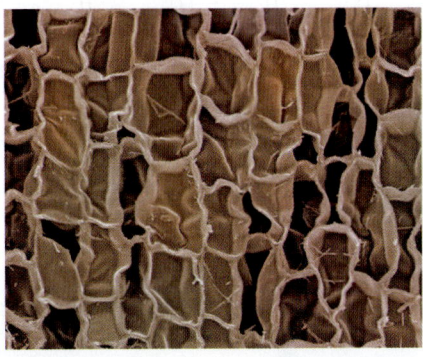
Cork is made up of dead cells.

Later, having built his own simple microscopes, **Anton van Leeuwenhoek** (1632–1723) observed and described cells such as red blood cells and spermatozoa. He was recognised as the discoverer of the microbial world for his observations of protozoa, microscopic algae, yeast and bacteria, which he called **animalcules** or 'small animals'.

SIMPLE MICROSCOPE
This consists of a tiny aspherical lens. Although not easy to use, it has high magnification power and can manage between 50 and 300 magnifications.

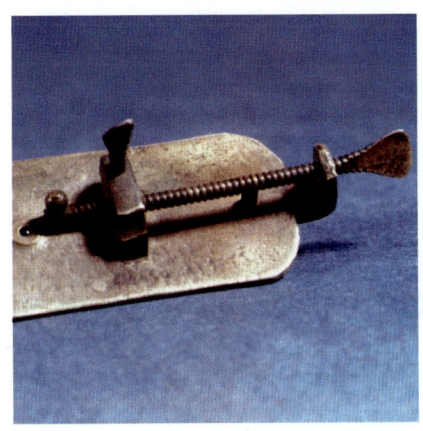

COMPOUND MICROSCOPE
This is based on the combination of various lenses, essentially three: objective, eyepiece and condenser. It is easy to use and can manage up to 2 000 magnifications.

ELECTRON MICROSCOPE
This was invented in the 1930s. Light is replaced by a beam of electrons and electromagnetic fields are used instead of lenses. It can manage up to a million magnifications.

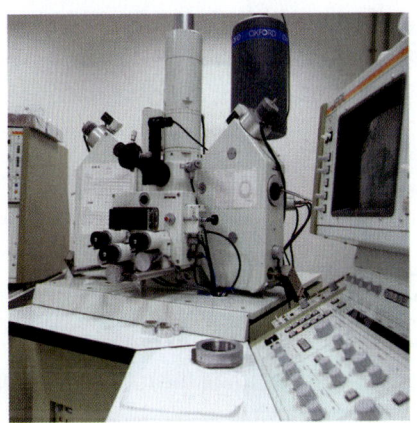

ACTIVITIES

3. Look for more information on the invention of the microscope and write a short report about it.

4. Mention the similarities and differences between:
   - the simple microscope and the compound microscope.
   - the electron microscope and the compound microscope.

5. What level of magnification can be achieved with the simple microscope? And with the compound microscope?

6. Did Robert Hooke really observe cells? Explain your answer.

7. Do you think that the animalcules that Leeuwenhoek described were small animals? What current groups of organisms was Leeuwenhoek referring to?

8. Explain why the discovery of the microscope was so important for biology.

2.1 Cell theory

In the 19th century, the German zoologist **Theodor Schwann** (1810–1882) and the German botanist **Matthias Schleiden** (1804–1881) started developing cell theory, which states that all living things are formed of cells.

This theory was expanded upon by **Rudolf Virchow** (1821–1902), who proved that cells reproduce, or rather all cells come from another cell. Meanwhile, the Spanish histologist **Santiago Ramón y Cajal** (1852–1934) established that **neurons** are independent cells, in this way stating that cell theory could also be applied to nervous tissue.

▲ Rudolf Virchow

▲ Santiago Ramón y Cajal

BASIC PRINCIPLES OF CELL THEORY
- All living things are made up of cells.
- All cells come from other pre-existing cells.
- All cells carry out the vital functions of living things: nutrition, reproduction and interaction.
- All cells contain the genetic information necessary to regulate cell functions and transmit this information to their descendants.

ACTIVITIES

9. Decide which of the following statements are false and explain why.
   a. A compound optical microscope is formed of two simple microscopes.
   b. Matthias Schleiden argued that not all living things are made up of cells.
   c. Matthias Schleiden and Theodor Schwann started the development of cell theory.
   d. Two thousand magnifications are possible with an electron microscope.
   e. Rudolf Virchow proved that cell theory could be applied to the nervous system.

10. Who was the researcher that came up with the idea that all cells arise from another cell?

11. What was Ramón y Cajal's main contribution to the establishment of cell theory?

12. Search for information about Ramón y Cajal and write a short report including:
    - Biographical data
    - Fields of research
    - Contributions to science

13. According to cell theory, why do you think viruses are not considered living things?

14. Given that cell theory was established before the electron microscope was invented, why was this invention so important for biology?

3. The organisation of living matter

> What does the endosymbiotic theory state?

All living things are composed of one or more cells. Living things made up of a single cell are called **unicellular organisms**. Those which are formed of groups of cells organised to varying degrees are **multicellular organisms**. In both cases, cells have a similar structure and individually carry out the **vital functions**.

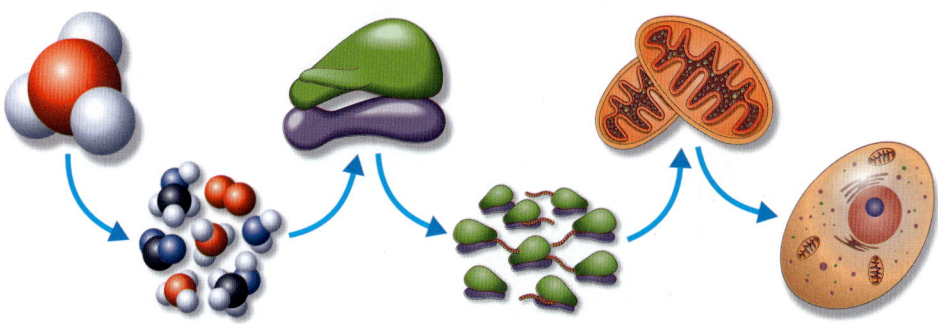

Living matter is organised into successive stages of complexity, from subatomic particles and atoms to cellular organisation. A complex combination of carbon, hydrogen, oxygen and nitrogen atoms create molecules and macromolecules. In turn, these molecules join up to form structures and organelles surrounded by a covering with the ability to reproduce and self-supply: the **cell**.

CELLS: THE UNITS OF LIFE

CELL SHAPE
Despite their structural and functional similarity, cells come in a wide variety of shapes and sizes, inhabit different environments and are either isolated or form part of complex organisms.

CELL SIZE
The diameter of the majority of cells varies between 0.5 and 20 microns, although there are cells which are substantially larger: the yolk of bird eggs and reptile eggs are very large ova.

CELL STRUCTURE
All cells have a basic common structure and the necessary equipment to obtain materials from the environment and generate new identical cells. This structure has three main components:

- **Plasma membrane**. This is a layer which surrounds the cell. It is through this membrane that the cell exchanges matter, energy and information with its outside.
- **Cytoplasm**. This is a thick fluid, **encased** by the plasma membrane. It is where organelles and other different molecules involved in various chemical reactions are found.
- **Genetic material**. This is made up of one or several nucleic acid molecules, and is the cell component that controls cell functions. It also stores and transfers hereditary information.

ACTIVITIES

15. What are the similarities between unicellular and multicellular living things?

16. The diameter of the majority of cells varies between 0.5 and 20 microns. Express these measurements in centimetres.

3.1 Models of cellular organisation

Depending on the way in which genetic material is contained within the cells, there are two models of cellular organisation: prokaryotic and eukaryotic.

PROKARYOTIC CELLS
These do not have a nuclear membrane and the genetic material is dispersed inside the cytoplasm.

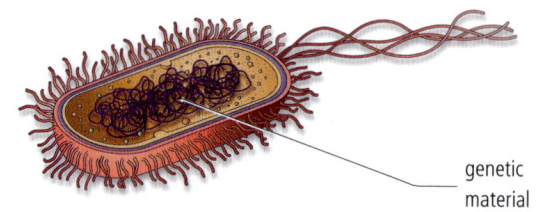

genetic material

EUKARYOTIC CELLS
These have a double nuclear membrane that separates the genetic material from the cytoplasm. They are bigger than prokaryotic cells.

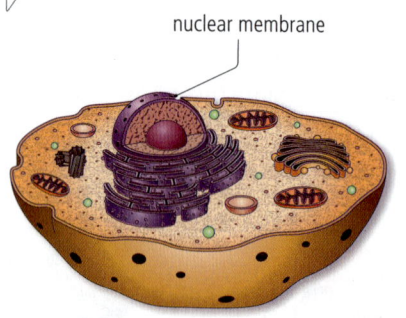

nuclear membrane

THE EVOLUTION OF PROKARYOTIC AND EUKARYOTIC CELLS

The oldest known fossils are prokaryotic cells that are approximately 3 500 m years old. The fossils of eukaryotic cells are more recent: the oldest known date back some 1 800 m years. There are several theories which attempt to explain the evolution of eukaryotic cells from prokaryotic ones.

One of these theories states that the nuclear membrane that surrounds the genetic material could have arisen from the plasma membrane folding inwards into the cytoplasm in an ancient prokaryotic cell, as in the following process:

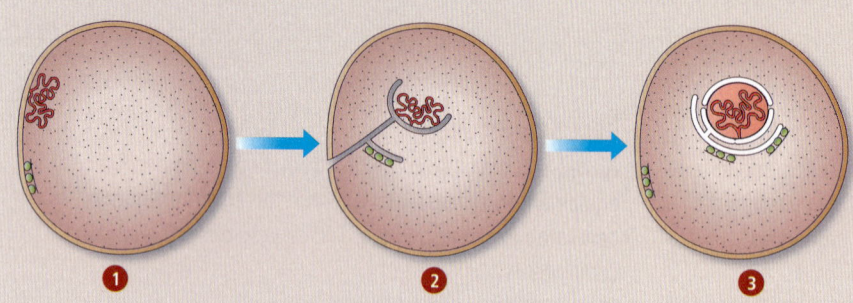

1 The original prokaryotic cell would have had its genetic material joined to the plasma membrane.

2 The membrane would have folded inwards and dragged the genetic material towards the middle of the cell.

3 The inward fold would have ended up surrounding the genetic material entirely, thus forming the nucleus.

In 1967, the American biologist Lynn Margulis (1938–2011) presented her theory on **endosymbiosis** to explain the origin of certain cellular organelles. This hypothesis states that it is very probable that organelles such as mitochondria originated from bacteria that were captured by a larger ancestral anaerobic prokaryotic cell.

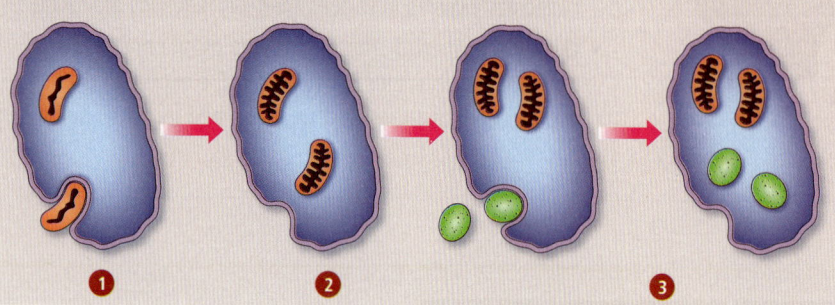

1 A large anaerobic prokaryotic cell captures an aerobic prokaryotic cell.

2 A symbiotic relationship forms between both cells: the captured cell obtains refuge and food in exchange for producing energy through aerobic respiration.

3 Chloroplasts would have had a similar origin: the incorporation of **cyanobacteria** would have created photosynthetic eukaryotic cells.

ACTIVITIES

17. Look for the etymological meaning of the terms *eukaryote* and *prokaryote*.

4 Prokaryotic cells

> What are the differences between a nucleus and a nucleoid?

The prokaryotic cellular organisation model is the most primitive. Prokaryotes are unicellular organisms, like **bacteria**.

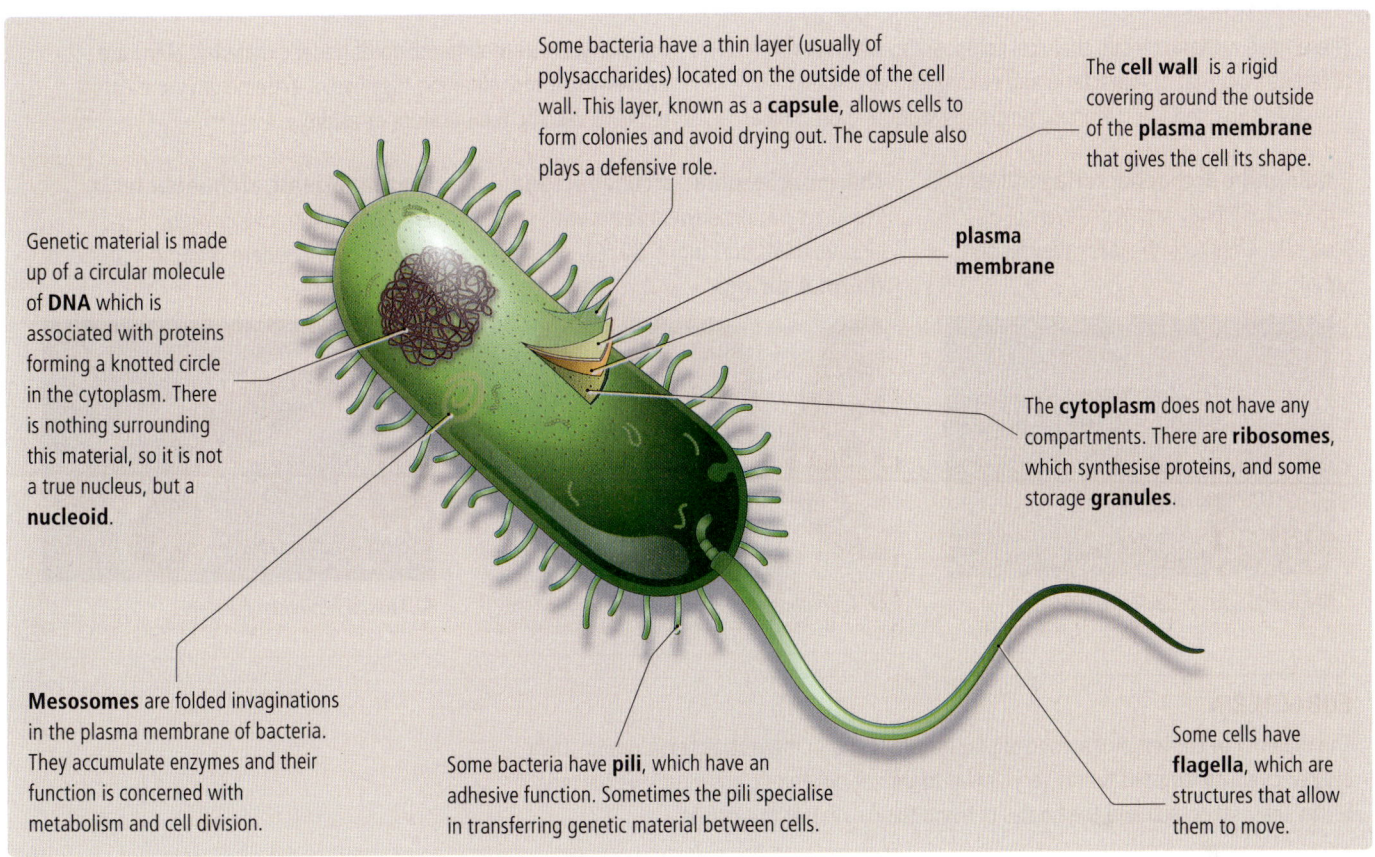

Some bacteria have a thin layer (usually of polysaccharides) located on the outside of the cell wall. This layer, known as a **capsule**, allows cells to form colonies and avoid drying out. The capsule also plays a defensive role.

The **cell wall** is a rigid covering around the outside of the **plasma membrane** that gives the cell its shape.

plasma membrane

Genetic material is made up of a circular molecule of **DNA** which is associated with proteins forming a knotted circle in the cytoplasm. There is nothing surrounding this material, so it is not a true nucleus, but a **nucleoid**.

The **cytoplasm** does not have any compartments. There are **ribosomes**, which synthesise proteins, and some storage **granules**.

Mesosomes are folded invaginations in the plasma membrane of bacteria. They accumulate enzymes and their function is concerned with metabolism and cell division.

Some bacteria have **pili**, which have an adhesive function. Sometimes the pili specialise in transferring genetic material between cells.

Some cells have **flagella**, which are structures that allow them to move.

CELLULAR FORMS OF PROKARYOTIC ORGANISMS

The cells of prokaryotic organisms may be spherical, rod-shaped or spiral. Sometimes prokaryotic cells join together creating small differently-shaped **colonies**.

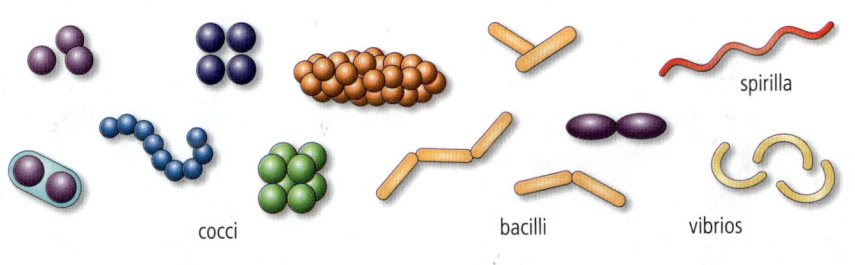

cocci   bacilli   vibrios   spirilla

ACTIVITIES

18. What is the function of the bacterial capsule? And that of the cell wall?

19. What is the difference between cocci, bacilli, vibrios and spirilla?

20. Are pili the same as flagella? Explain your answer.

21. Develop a theory that explains why the DNA in the nucleoid is rolled up in the form of a knotted circle. Then compare your theory with the different hypotheses that your classmates have developed.

4.1 Bacteria

Prokaryotic organisms are bacteria. Depending on the chemical composition of their membranes and cell walls, they are divided into two groups: archaebacteria and eubacteria.

ARCHAEBACTERIA

These have a characteristic chemical composition which is very different from that of eubacteria and eukaryotic cells. They resemble eubacteria in metabolic processes, but are more similar to eukaryotes in their handling of genetic material. Many are **extremophiles**, meaning they live in extreme environments in terms of salinity, temperature or acidity.

Halophilic archaebacteria proliferate in environments with high levels of salinity. They turn the lakes they inhabit pink.

▲ Owens Lake in California (USA)

Thermoacidophilic archaebacteria live in very acidic environments with high temperatures (up to 80 °C), such as **thermal springs**.

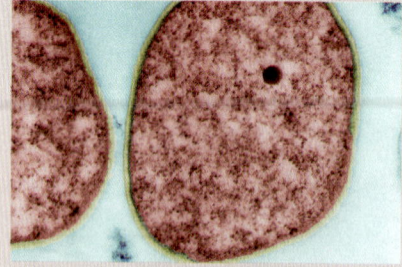

▲ Sulfolobus acidocaldarius

Methanogenic archaebacteria are plentiful in low-oxygen environments where organic material is decomposing.

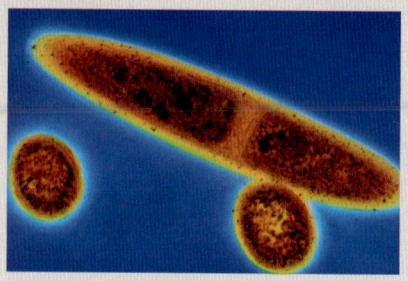

▲ Methanospirillum hungatii

EUBACTERIA

The majority of current prokaryotic organisms are found in the **eubacteria** group. Their cellular chemical composition is very similar to that of eukaryotic organisms. Eubacteria live in seas, lakes, soil and the bodies of living things all over the planet.

Enteric bacteria are found in the intestines of mammals. They live in symbiosis with their hosts: bacteria avoid the proliferation of pathogenic microorganisms and, in turn, receive nutrients from the host's digestion.

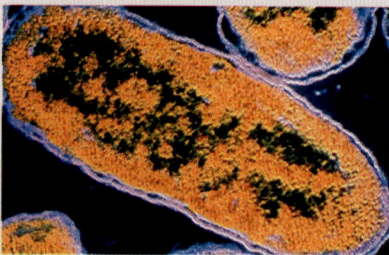

▲ Escherichia coli

Many **heterotrophic bacteria**, known as aerobic because they need oxygen to survive, decompose dead matter and the remains of organic matter and convert them into inorganic matter that can be used by autotrophic organisms.

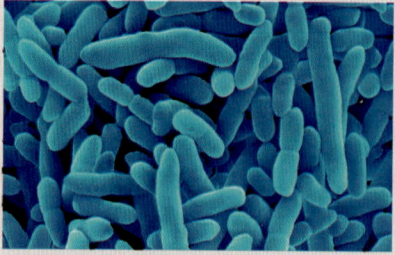

▲ Pseudomonas putida

Cyanobacteria or **blue-green algae** sometimes form multicellular filaments. They are responsible for the accumulation of oxygen in the atmosphere through photosynthesis. They are larger than other prokaryotes.

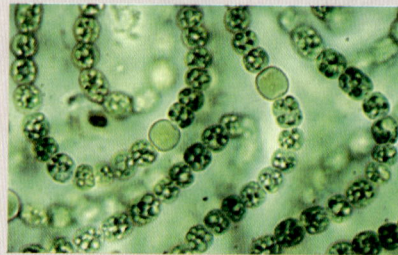

▲ Nostoc commune

ACTIVITIES

22. Summarise the cell forms and cell associations that occur in prokaryotic organisms.

23. There are two different groups of prokaryotic organisms. What are they? What do researchers base this difference on?

5. Eukaryotic cells

> Do plant cells have centrosomes?

The majority of living things in the biosphere have eukaryotic cells. The eukaryotic cellular organisation model appears in unicellular organisms such as protozoa, in unicellular or multicellular organisms like algae and fungi, and in multicellular organisms such as plants and animals.

In terms of their nutrition, relationships and reproduction, there are two models of eukaryotic cells: **animal cells** and **plant cells**. These two types of cells have multiple structures and organelles in common. They also have their own specific organelles and structures.

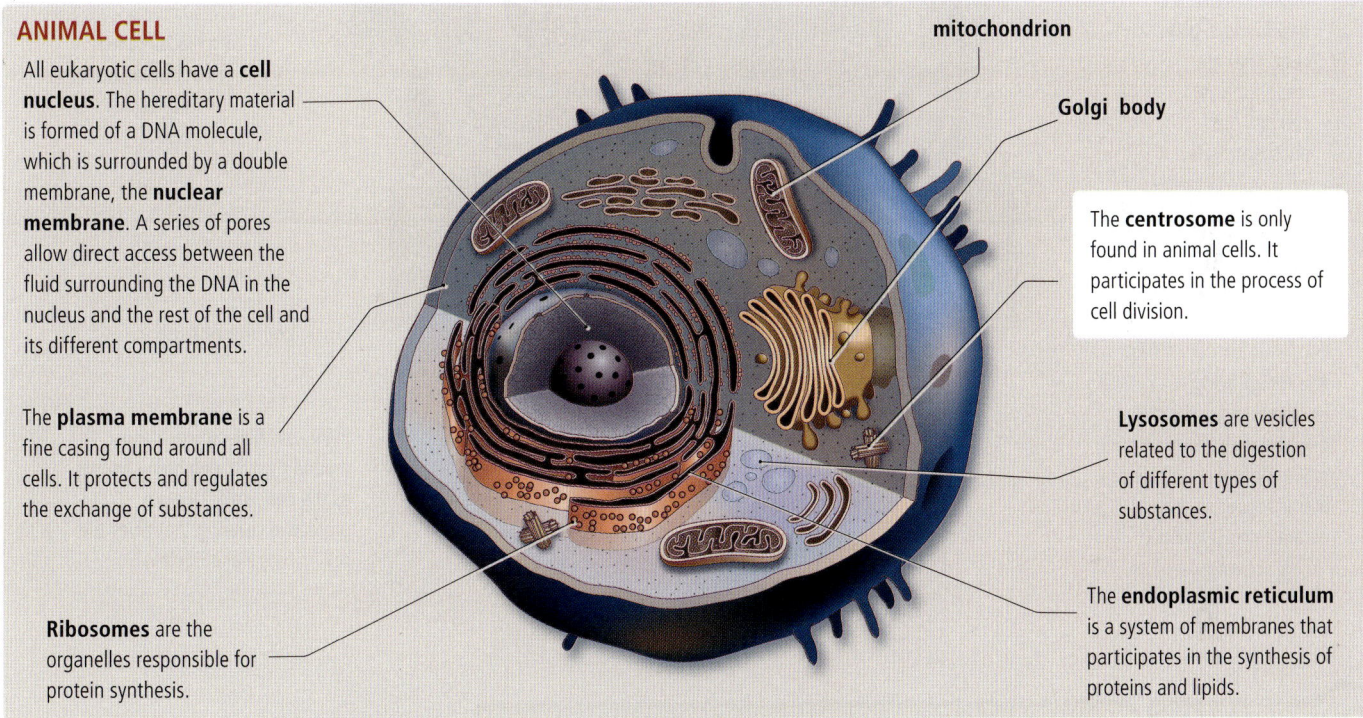

ANIMAL CELL

All eukaryotic cells have a **cell nucleus**. The hereditary material is formed of a DNA molecule, which is surrounded by a double membrane, the **nuclear membrane**. A series of pores allow direct access between the fluid surrounding the DNA in the nucleus and the rest of the cell and its different compartments.

The **plasma membrane** is a fine casing found around all cells. It protects and regulates the exchange of substances.

Ribosomes are the organelles responsible for protein synthesis.

mitochondrion

Golgi body

The **centrosome** is only found in animal cells. It participates in the process of cell division.

Lysosomes are vesicles related to the digestion of different types of substances.

The **endoplasmic reticulum** is a system of membranes that participates in the synthesis of proteins and lipids.

CELLULAR FORMS OF EUKARYOTIC ORGANISMS

Eukaryotic cells can be prism-shaped, such as the epithelial cells of animals and the majority of plant cells. There are also star-shaped cells, such as neurons and bone tissue cells. Muscle cells are usually elongated and **spindle-shaped**. Erythrocytes (red blood cells) are disc-shaped cells.

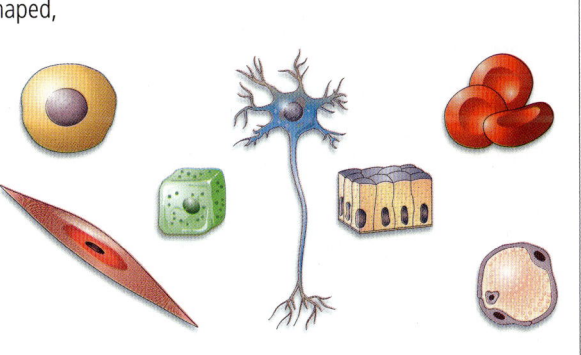

ACTIVITIES

24. Is the eukaryotic cellular organisation model exclusive to multicellular organisms? Explain your answer.

UNIT 01 Cells: the basic units of life

PLANT CELL

Eukaryotic cells have a much more complex **cytoplasm** than prokaryotic cells. Their cytoplasm contains numerous **cell organelles** to carry out specific functions in the cell. They also have a **cytoskeleton** which gives the cells their shape and helps them to move.

Chloroplasts are organelles that are only found in plant cells. They are responsible for carrying out photosynthesis.

The **Golgi body** is a system of membranous vesicles involved in the transport and maturation of the molecules manufactured in the endoplasmic reticulum.

Vacuoles are large membranous organelles which are found in both animal and plant cells but are much larger in plant cells. They are involved in storing different substances and maintaining cellular turgidity.

All eukaryotic cells have organelles called **mitochondria**. These carry out cellular respiration.

cell membrane

Plant cells have an envelope around the cell membrane known as the **cell wall**. This is a protective covering that gives the cell its shape and rigidity.

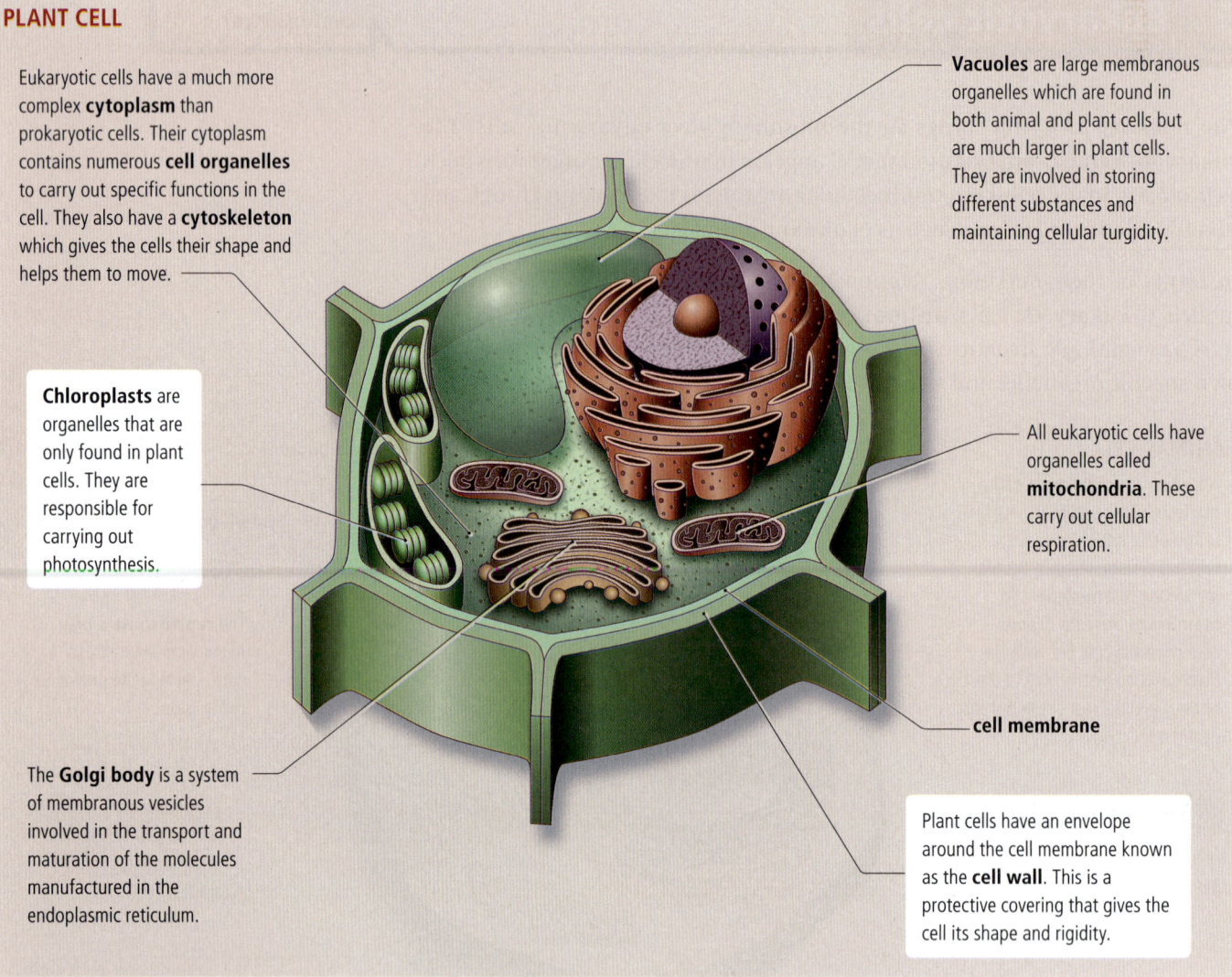

ACTIVITIES

25. Make a table to compare the structure of prokayotic and eukaryotic cells.

26. Indicate which type of cellular organisation (eukaryotic or prokaryotic) these organelles or structures belong to:
  a. mesosome
  b. ribosome
  c. centrosome
  d. pili
  e. nucleus
  e. cell wall
  f. capsule
  g. mitochondria
  h. chloroplast
  i. Golgi body

27. Through which structures does the inside of the nucleus come into contact with the rest of the cell?

28. Develop a theory that explains the presence of the cell wall in plant cells and its absence in animal cells.

29. Which eukaryotic cell organelles are similar to bacteria? This fact has helped some scientists to develop theories on the evolution of eukaryotic and prokaryotic cells. Briefly explain some of them.

6. Components of eukaryotic cells

> Where is cellular respiration performed?

Eukaryotic cells are more complex than prokaryotic cells and have different structures and organelles.

6.1 Plasma membrane

The plasma membrane, also known as the **cell membrane**, is a fine casing found around all cells. It protects and regulates the exchange of substances between the cytoplasm and the outside of the cell.

PLASMA MEMBRANE STRUCTURE

The membrane **proteins** can be immersed in the double layer or just attached to one of the layers. Some proteins of the membrane act as **stimulant receptors**.

A **double layer** of **lipid** molecules interspersed with protein molecules.

The plasma membrane is fluid, given that its molecules have the ability to rotate and move laterally. Its degree of fluidity depends on the type of lipids that it is comprised of. In animal cells, this fluidity is controlled by **cholesterol** molecules, which, inserted between the rest of the lipids, make it relatively rigid.

THE EXCHANGE OF SUBSTANCES THROUGH THE PLASMA MEMBRANE

Depending on its size and nature, matter enters and leaves the cells through the cell membrane. It uses different mechanisms to enter; there are molecules such as CO_2 and O_2 and ions like Na^+ and K^+ that pass directly into the cell by **diffusion**. Water passes in and out of the cell by **osmosis**.

Other ways for substances to pass through the plasma membrane are as follows:

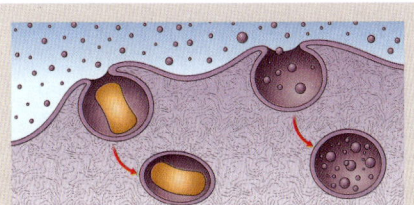

Endocytosis is a process in which the cell captures large substances. It consists of the formation of an inward fold or invagination of the membrane towards the inside of the cell.

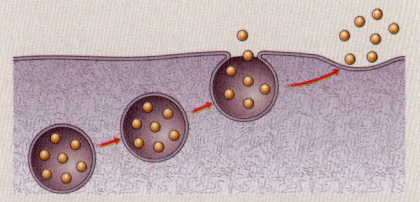

Exocytosis is a process similar to endocytosis but works in the reverse way. Insoluble or large molecules are expelled from the cell to the outside.

Permeases are proteins that transport substances across the membrane; when they do it against a concentration gradient, the process consumes energy.

ACTIVITIES

30. What substances are the plasma membranes of all living things made up of?

31. Do you think that cholesterol is harmful for our organism? Justify your answer.

32. Compare endocytosis and exocytosis and explain the differences between the two processes.

33. Look for information on the processes of diffusion and osmosis in cells and briefly explain them.

6.2 Cell wall

In tissues, cells join up with each other by means of the substances that they secrete and which occupy the spaces between them. These substances make up what is known as the **extracellular matrix**. The **cell wall** is a type of extracellular matrix of plant cells. Sometimes, certain compounds accumulate, for example, lignin, which gives woody plants their typical rigidity.

CELL WALL STRUCTURE

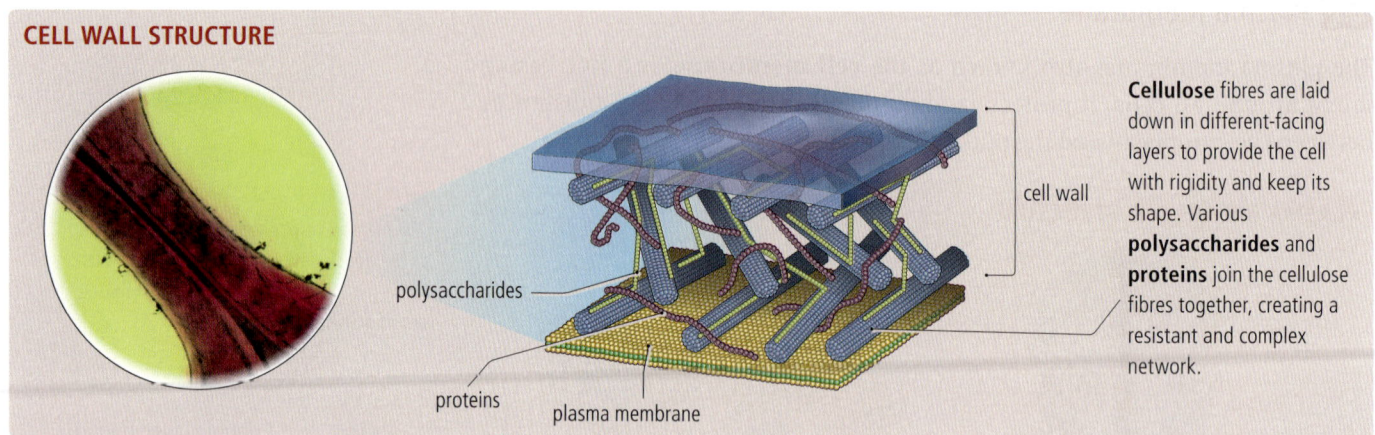

Cellulose fibres are laid down in different-facing layers to provide the cell with rigidity and keep its shape. Various **polysaccharides** and **proteins** join the cellulose fibres together, creating a resistant and complex network.

6.3 Cytoplasm

The **cytoplasm** is the total content between the cell nucleus and the plasma membrane. It is made up of a watery medium called the **cytosol**. This is where the **cytoskeleton**, cell organelles and also the protein, amino-acid, carbohydrate, lipid and mineral-salt molecules involved in the different chemical reactions occurring inside the cells are suspended. The cytosol takes up half of the cell's volume, the other half being organelles and the membranous vesicles of the endoplasmic reticulum and the Golgi body.

> Some free cells that do not have rigid membranes, such as amoebas and white blood cells, have extensions of the cytoplasm that allow them to move: **pseudopods**. This movement, called **amoeboid movement,** is possible because of the coordinated activity of protein fibres of the cytoskeleton.

CYTOSKELETON

The cytoskeleton gives the cell its shape, allows it to make different movements, transports materials from one area of the cell to another, and participates in the movement and organisation of the different organelles in the cytoplasm.

The cytoskeleton is organised as a complex network of interconnected protein filaments. The connections between the subunits are weak, allowing them to be quickly assembled and disassembled. There are three types of filaments: microtubules, microfilaments and intermediate filaments.

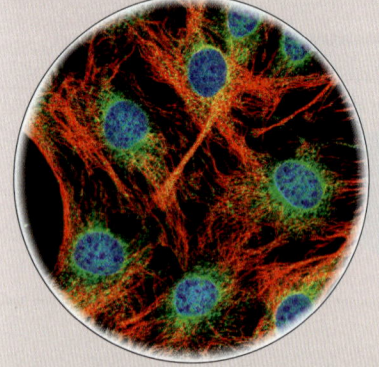
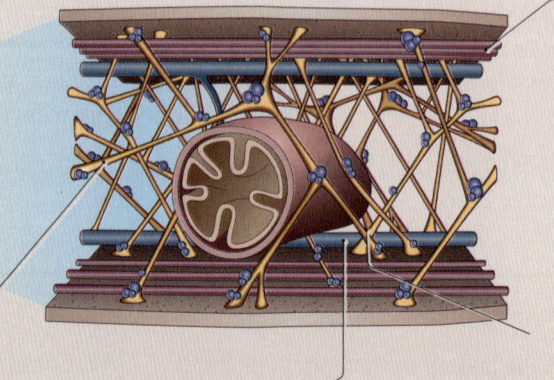

Microfilaments are polymers made from a protein called **actin**. Grouped in double helices, these polymers form bundles and networks throughout the cytoplasm, although they are more concentrated around the plasma membrane. They are thin and break easily.

Intermediate filaments are made up of polymerised protein subunits similar to ropes. They are easy to construct, but difficult to break.

Microtubules are polymers made from the protein **tubulin**, which forms hollow and very rigid cylindrical structures.

6.4 Cell organelles

CENTROSOME

The centrosome, found only in animal cells, is an organelle that stays close to the nucleus when the cell is at rest. Before the cell divides, the centrosome duplicates itself and the two fractions move apart until they are on opposite poles of the cell.

The function of the centrosome is related to the formation and organisation of the cytoskeleton and, like the cytoskeleton, is also formed of proteins. Similarly, it is involved in the movement of the cell by cilia and flagella, and participates actively in the process of cell division, forming the mitotic spindle.

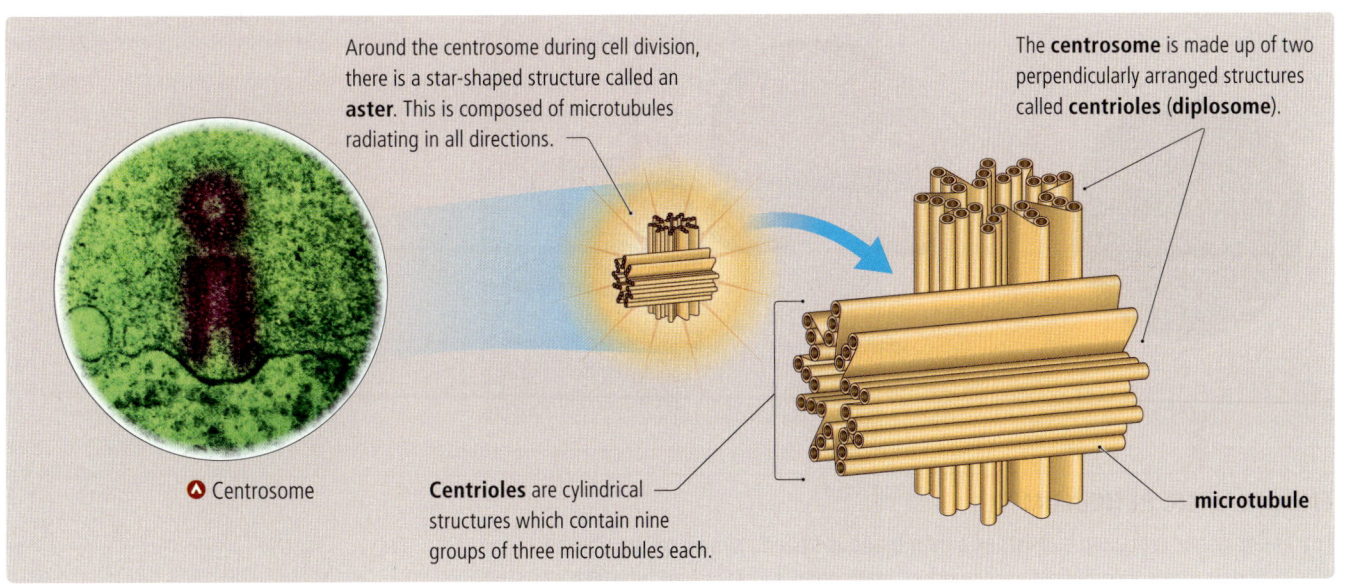

Around the centrosome during cell division, there is a star-shaped structure called an **aster**. This is composed of microtubules radiating in all directions.

The **centrosome** is made up of two perpendicularly arranged structures called **centrioles** (**diplosome**).

 Centrosome

Centrioles are cylindrical structures which contain nine groups of three microtubules each.

microtubule

ACTIVITIES

34. What are permeases? Where can they be found?
35. What are the similarities and differences between the processes of osmosis and diffusion?
36. Explain the function of cellulose in the cells of plants.
37. Is the cell wall the same as the plasma membrane? Explain your answer.
38. Explain the relationship between the cytoskeleton and the centrosome.
39. What are the differences between the cytoplasm, the cytosol and the cytoskeleton?
40. List the main functions of the cytoskeleton.
41. What do intermediate filaments, microfilaments and microtubules have in common?
42. Decide whether the following statements are true or false and correct the false ones:
    a. Microtubules involved in the cell's inside movement are organised by a cellular body known as the cytoskeleton.
    b. The centrosome of animal cells is made up of two centrioles whereas the centrosome of plant cells is made up of one centriole which contains nine groups of three microtubules.

RIBOSOMES

Ribosomes are organelles located in the cytosol. They are attached to the membranes of the endoplasmic reticulum or inside other organelles, such as mitochondria and chloroplasts. They are larger in eukaryotic cells than in prokaryotic ones. Prokaryotic ribosomes are similar to those which appear in mitochondria and chloroplasts.

The function of ribosomes is to make cell proteins from the information provided by the nucleic acids.

> **RNA**
>
> RNA, or **ribonucleic acid**, is related to DNA in terms of its chemical nature and its function. There are three types: **messenger RNA** (mRNA), ribosomal RNA (**rRNA**) and **transfer RNA** (tRNA). Each has the same purpose: so that the hereditary information contained in the DNA is expressed in the cells.

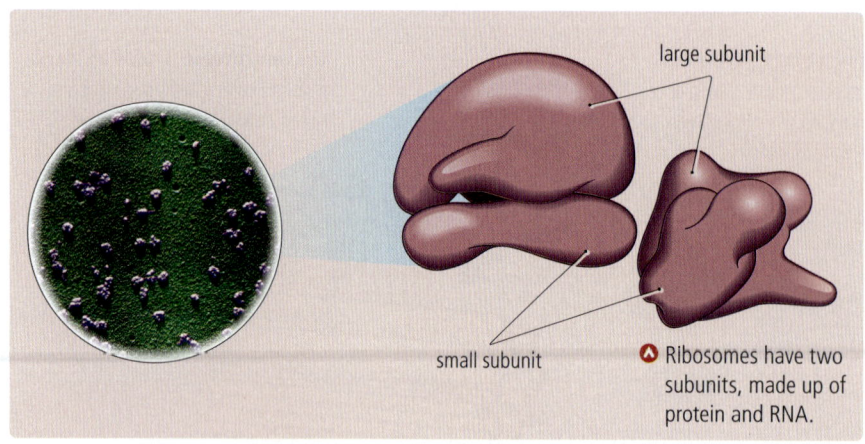

Ribosomes have two subunits, made up of protein and RNA.

ENDOPLASMIC RETICULUM

The endoplasmic reticulum consists of a membranous system, similar to the plasma membrane. It forms a complicated network of interconnected sacs and tube-like structures, which are also connected with the Golgi body and the nuclear membrane.

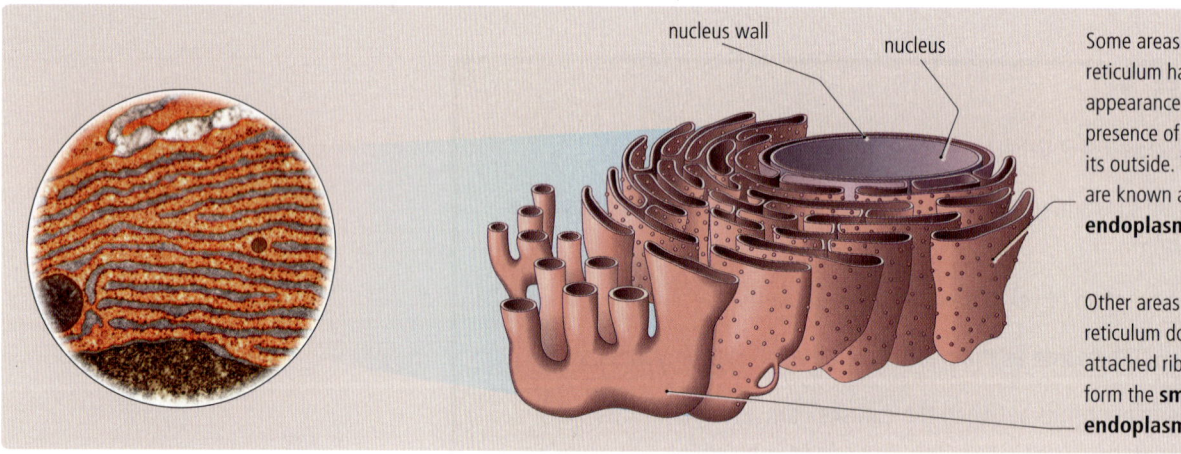

Some areas of the reticulum have a rough appearance because of the presence of ribosomes on its outside. These areas are known as the **rough endoplasmic reticulum**.

Other areas of the reticulum do not have any attached ribosomes and form the **smooth endoplasmic reticulum**.

The rough endoplasmic reticulum is involved in the synthesis of proteins. These proteins will form part of the membranes of the reticulum, the plasma membrane and the membranes of other organelles. Some proteins will also be exported outside the cell.

The smooth endoplasmic reticulum participates in the synthesis of lipids, which will also be incorporated into different membranous systems in the cell.

ACTIVITIES

43. Where are ribosomes located in eukaryotic cells? What is their function?

44. Explain the similarities and differences between the rough and the smooth endoplasmic reticulum.

GOLGI BODY

The Golgi body is made up of a stack of disc-shaped membranous sacs close to the nucleus. Together with these discs, there is a series of vesicles which vary in size depending on the side of the body they are on. On the side closest to the nucleus or *cis* face, these vesicles are smaller than on the side which faces the plasma membrane, known as the *trans* face.

The Golgi body produces the majority of the cell's **polysaccharides**. The sorting and maturation of the proteins and lipids from the endoplasmic reticulum also takes place here. This maturation occurs while these molecules are being transported from the *cis* face to the *trans* face. Then, they are packaged into vesicles to be secreted to the outside or distributed among different places inside the cell.

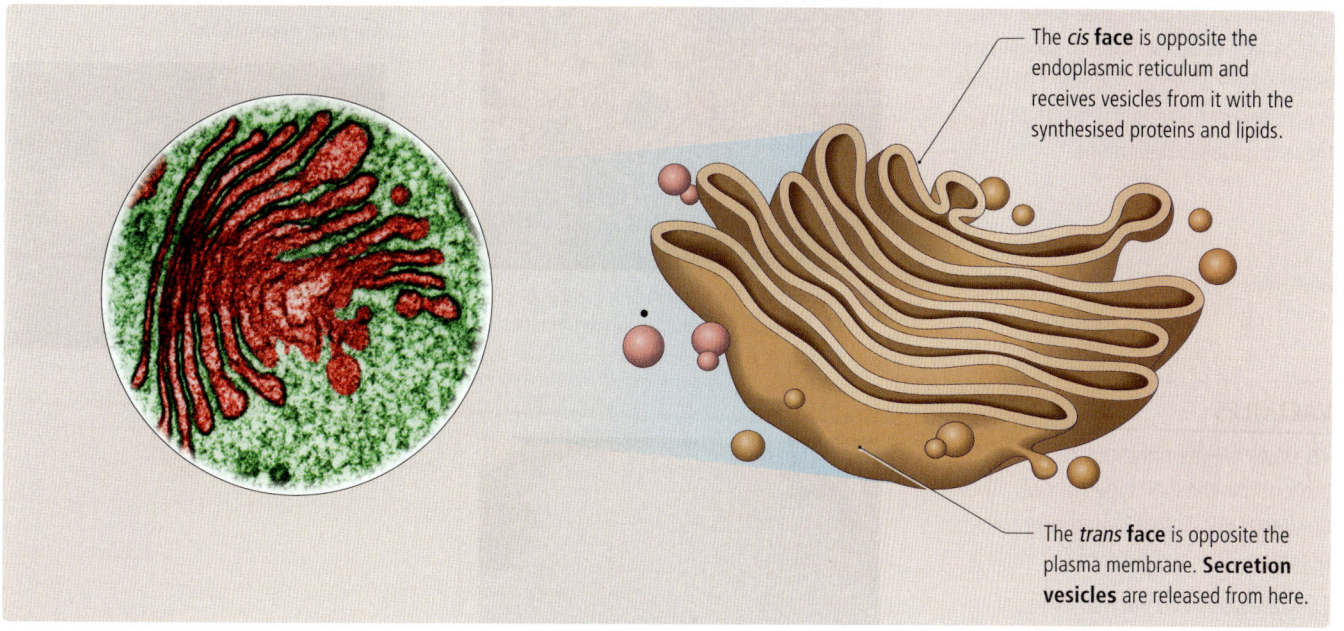

The *cis* **face** is opposite the endoplasmic reticulum and receives vesicles from it with the synthesised proteins and lipids.

The *trans* **face** is opposite the plasma membrane. **Secretion vesicles** are released from here.

LYSOSOMES

Lysosomes are vesicles from the Golgi body that contain acidic digestive enzymes. These enzymes digest materials from the outside or the inside of the cell, such as its own waste, food particles or **phagocytised** microorganisms. This compartmentalisation of digestive enzymes protects the cytosol from being attacked by its own digestive system.

The membrane of lysosomes has transporter proteins. These allow the end products of the digestion to be released into the cytosol, to be either reused or excreted by the cell.

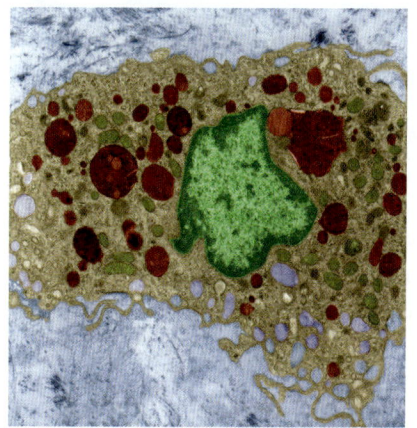

⬥ Lysosomes contain enzymes for intracellular digestion of macromolecules.

ACTIVITIES

45. What is the relationship between the endoplasmic reticulum and the Golgi body?

46. Explain the difference between the *cis* and *trans* faces of the Golgi body, and describe what happens in each.

47. Describe the structure and function of lysosomes.

PEROXISOMES

Peroxisomes are organelles surrounded by a single membrane. They are found in nearly all types of eukaryotic cells. Together with mitochondria, they are the main cell compartments which use oxygen. Peroxisomes are responsible for the oxidation reactions that allow toxic substances to be eliminated. Oxygenated water, also known as hydrogen peroxide, is involved in these reactions, thus giving these organelles their name.

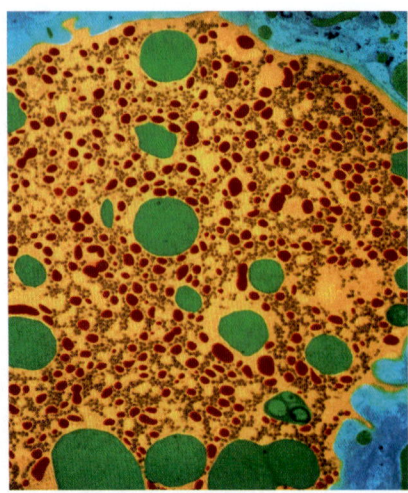

Peroxisomes are in abundance in hepatic cells because of their detoxifying function.

DID YOU KNOW?

Proteins, fats and carbohydrates are safely stored in the vacuoles of storage cells in seeds for many years. These macromolecules will be used when germination takes place. Vegetative reproduction by tubers, rhizomes and bulbs depends to a large extent on this storage of food material in vacuoles for the next generation.

VACUOLES

Vacuoles are membranous organelles present in almost all types of cells. They are larger in plant cells, and take up between 30% and 90% of cell volume.

They are similar to the lysosomes of animal cells in that they contain numerous enzymes, although they carry out more functions.

Plant vacuoles store water and various substances that the cell must eliminate, assimilate, digest or reserve. They are also related to the effective increase in cell volume, meaning the cytoplasm content does not increase. They exert pressure on the cell wall, maintaining **turgidity** and stopping the plant from withering.

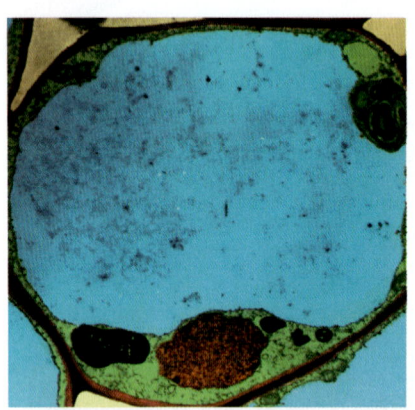

An electron micrograph of a plant cell containing a vacuole

One cell can contain several different vacuoles, each with different functions.

ACTIVITIES

48. What are the differences between lysosomes and vacuoles?

49. What is a peroxisome? What role does it play in the cell?

50. Are vacuole organelles found only in plant cells? Explain your answer.

51. Which eukaryotic organelle or cell component is in charge of the following functions?

   a. Produce oxidation reactions that allow toxic substances to be eliminated.

   b. Digest materials from the outside or inside of the cell (waste, food particles or microorganisms).

   c. Store water and various substances that the cell must eliminate, assimilate, digest or reserve.

   d. Produce the majority of the cell's polysaccharides and sort the proteins and lipids from the endoplasmic reticulum.

   e. Are involved in the formation and organisation of the cytoskeleton.

   f. Make cell proteins.

MITOCHONDRIA

Mitochondria are organelles which are located in the cytoplasm of all eukaryotic cells. They are surrounded by a double membrane.

Mitochondria are able to replicate themselves, which means that new mitochondria arise from the growth and division of others.

Mitochondria provide eukaryotic cells with their source of energy. Enzymes in the crests and the matrix are involved in cellular respiration. The energy the cell needs to carry out its vital functions is generated by this process.

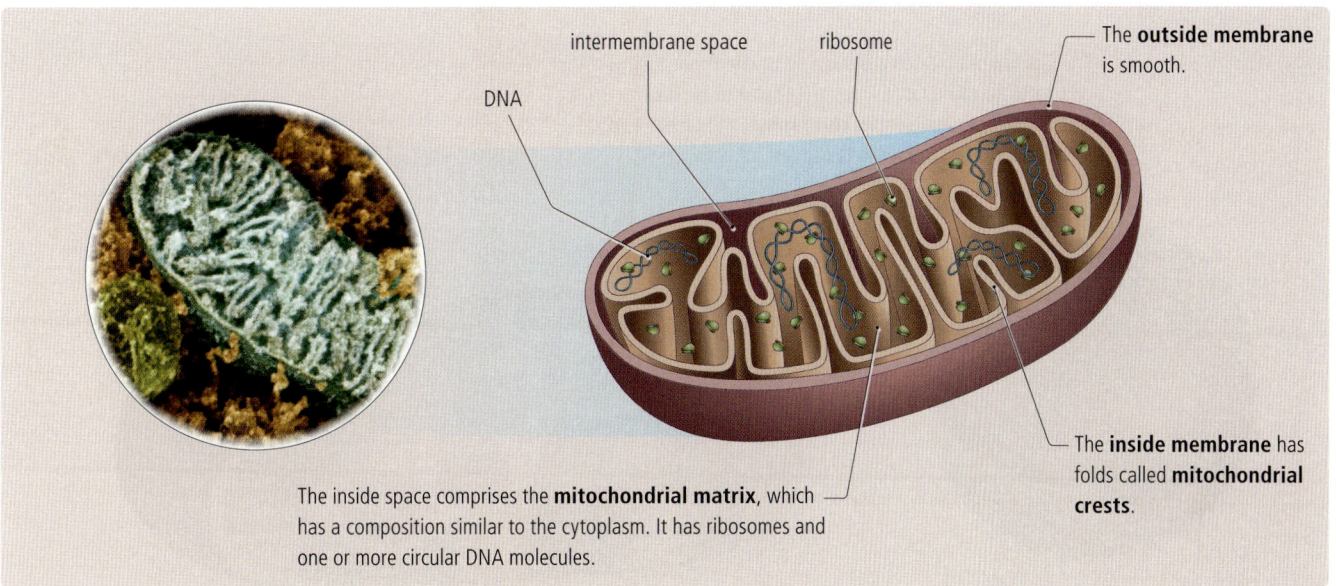

- intermembrane space
- ribosome
- DNA
- The **outside membrane** is smooth.
- The inside space comprises the **mitochondrial matrix**, which has a composition similar to the cytoplasm. It has ribosomes and one or more circular DNA molecules.
- The **inside membrane** has folds called **mitochondrial crests**.

MITOCHONDRIA AND CELL RESPIRATION

Cellular metabolism is the set of chemical reactions that occur inside the cell for it to survive, develop and reproduce. The metabolism consists of two types of interdependent phases: catabolism and anabolism.

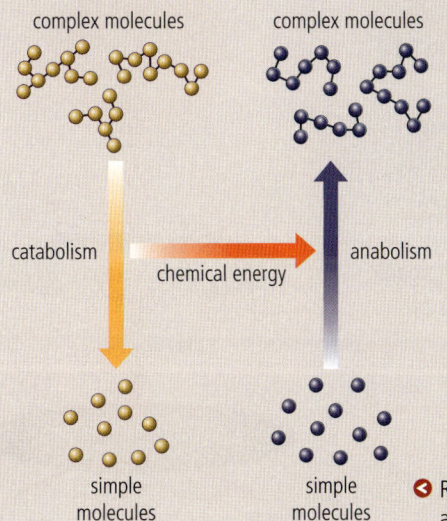

◀ Relationship between catabolic and anabolic processes

Catabolism. Complex molecules are broken down into other simpler molecules, releasing energy.

Anabolism. Complex molecules are created from other simpler molecules, requiring energy.

One of the most important catabolic cell processes is **cellular respiration**. This is the breakdown of organic fuels by molecular oxygen, giving the cell the energy that it needs. Some of the respiratory process reactions occur in the cytoplasm and the rest, inside the mitochondria. In simple terms, cellular respiration can be represented by the following chemical equation:

$$C_6H_{12}O_6 + 6\ O_2 \rightarrow 6\ CO_2 + 6\ H_2O + energy$$

Glucose ($C_6H_{12}O_6$), in the presence of oxygen (O_2) and by means of a series of **exothermic reactions**, is converted into carbon dioxide (CO_2) and water (H_2O). Energy is released.

ACTIVITIES

52. Why are mitochondria important for the cell?

53. What do the chemical reactions that occur in the mitochondria and the peroxisomes have in common?

54. Briefly describe cellular respiration.

55. Develop a theory on the role that DNA plays inside mitochondria.

CHLOROPLASTS

Chloroplasts are the most characteristic organelles in plant cells. They are surrounded by a double membrane.

Like mitochondria, chloroplasts have one or several circular copies of DNA which are able to replicate themselves. The function of chloroplasts is to carry out photosynthesis.

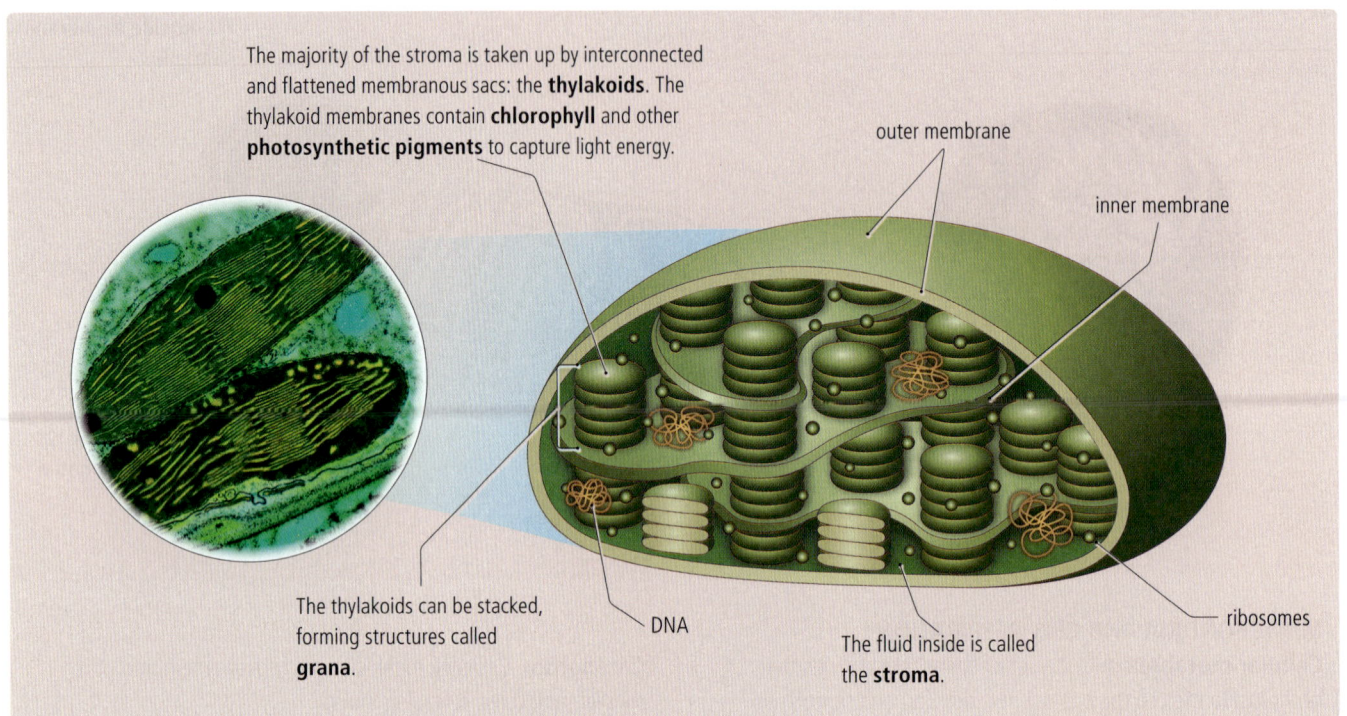

The majority of the stroma is taken up by interconnected and flattened membranous sacs: the **thylakoids**. The thylakoid membranes contain **chlorophyll** and other **photosynthetic pigments** to capture light energy.

outer membrane

inner membrane

The thylakoids can be stacked, forming structures called **grana**.

DNA

The fluid inside is called the **stroma**.

ribosomes

CHLOROPLASTS AND PHOTOSYNTHESIS

The main cellular anabolic process is photosynthesis, which is carried out in the chloroplasts. It consists of the conversion of inorganic matter into organic matter using solar light as a source of energy. Photosynthesis occurs in two stages:

- **Light reaction**. Electromagnetic light energy is transformed into chemical energy. Water molecules also separate into oxygen, which is released, and hydrogen, which is subsequently used. This process of breaking down water molecules is known as **hydrolysis**.
- **Dark reaction**. Organic material is synthesised in the form of **glucose** from inorganic material: carbon dioxide from the atmosphere and hydrogen from the hydrolysis of water. This phase consumes some of the energy obtained in the light reaction.

The chemical reactions that occur in photosynthesis can be simplified as follows:

$6\ CO_2 + 6\ H_2O + energy \rightarrow C_6H_{12}O_6 + 6\ O_2$

Carbon dioxide (CO_2) and water (H_2O), through different **endothermic reactions**, are converted into glucose ($C_6H_{12}O_6$) and oxygen (O_2) which is released.

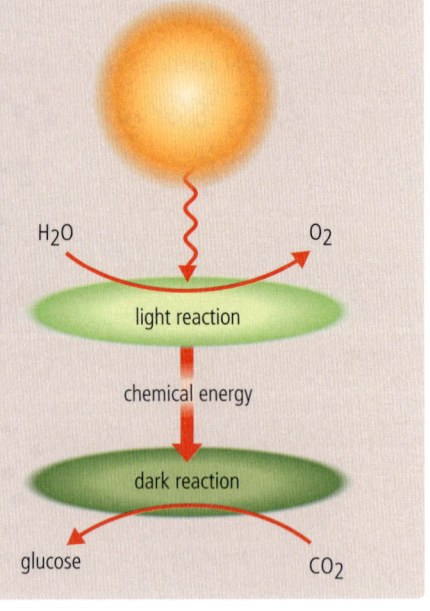

ACTIVITIES

56. What is the difference between light reaction and dark reaction in photosynthesis?

57. Draw a chloroplast and label its parts.

58. What are photosynthetic pigments? Where can they be found?

59. What do mitochondria and chloroplasts have in common?

6.5 The nucleus

The **nucleus** is a structure visible with a simple optical microscope. It contains the majority of a eukaryotic cell's genetic material.

The nucleus is responsible for controlling cell functions and is related to the transfer of traits between progenitors and their descendants. It is also the place where most DNA and RNA synthesis takes place.

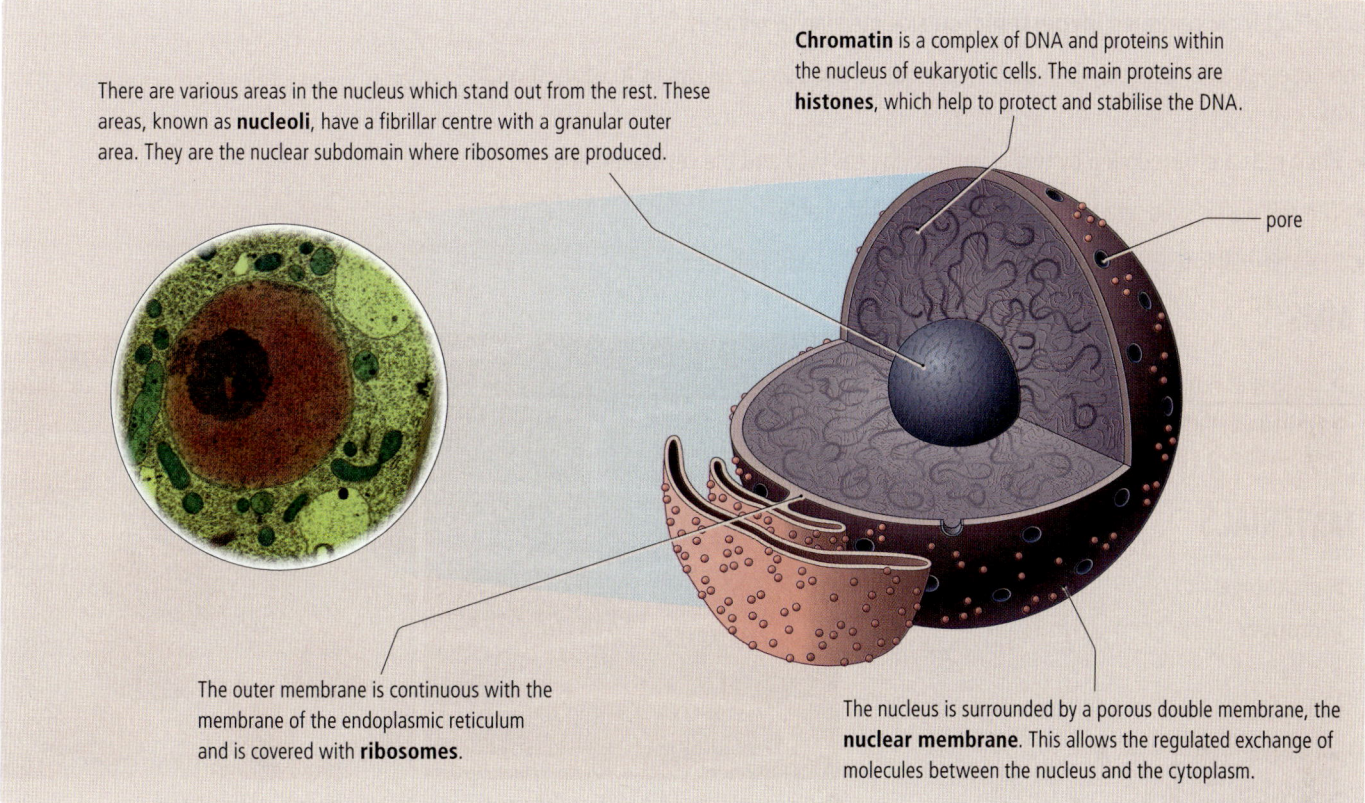

There are various areas in the nucleus which stand out from the rest. These areas, known as **nucleoli**, have a fibrillar centre with a granular outer area. They are the nuclear subdomain where ribosomes are produced.

Chromatin is a complex of DNA and proteins within the nucleus of eukaryotic cells. The main proteins are **histones**, which help to protect and stabilise the DNA.

pore

The outer membrane is continuous with the membrane of the endoplasmic reticulum and is covered with **ribosomes**.

The nucleus is surrounded by a porous double membrane, the **nuclear membrane**. This allows the regulated exchange of molecules between the nucleus and the cytoplasm.

ACTIVITIES

60. What is the function of the cell nucleus?

61. Rewrite any statements that are incorrect:
    a. All the DNA of eukaryotic cells is found in the nucleus.
    b. Plant cells do not need mitochondria to obtain energy through cellular respiration, as they make use of light energy.
    c. Photosynthetic pigments are found in the crests and matrices of mitochondria.
    d. The function of ribosomes is to synthesise all of the cell's nucleic acids.
    e. The endoplasmic reticulum has a *cis* face and a *trans* face.
    f. The absence of pores in the nuclear membrane isolates the nucleus from the rest of the cell.

62. Classify cell structures and organelles into two groups depending on whether they have membranes or not.

63. Search for information on the theory that attempts to explain the formation of the cell nucleus during the process of cell evolution.

BIG THINKER

The son of a Scottish church minister, **Robert Brown** collected plants as a child and became so engrossed with botany that he never completed his medical degree. Instead, he became a military surgeon's assistant, and later travelled to Australia, where he catalogued thousands of plant species not previously known to the scientific community. He is remembered for being the first person to name the nucleus in plant cells, which he observed even through quite primitive microscopes. Do you know of anyone else who abandoned their academic studies to become an expert in another field?

Discovery techniques

OBSERVING PLASMOLYSIS IN PLANT CELLS

> How can we observe the process of plasmolysis?

Plasmolysis is a process of cell destruction from dehydration. It happens as a result of water passing from the less concentrated solution inside the cell (**hypotonic medium**) to the highly concentrated (**hypertonic**) outside medium by osmosis.

The observation of plasmolysis in plant cells under a microscope allows us to verify several facts:

- Plant cells are surrounded by two coverings: the cell wall and the cell membrane.
- The cell wall is rigid and the cell membrane is deformable.
- The cell wall is fully permeable and the membrane is semi-permeable.

AIMS

> Observe plasmolysis.
> Distinguish the plasma membrane from the cell wall.

MATERIALS

> microscope
> **dropper**
> slide
> flower petals
> coverslip
> table salt
> beaker
> **distilled water**

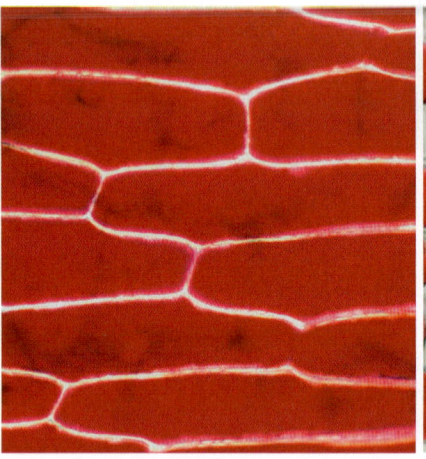 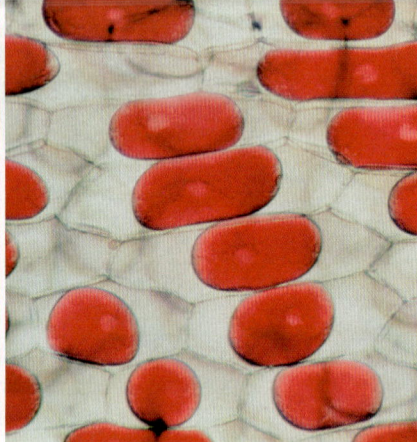

◯ Onion epidermal cells before (left) and after (right) plasmolysis; each cell contains a red-pigmented cytoplasm.

PROCEDURE

1. Take a coloured petal from a flower and separate the epidermis with some tweezers.
2. Dampen a piece of epidermis with water and place it on a slide. Observe this preparation under the microscope.
3. Next, place various drops of a solution of water saturated with sodium chloride onto the preparation.
4. Cover with a coverslip and observe the slide under the microscope again.

CONCLUSIONS

1. In your notebook, describe and draw what you observed before and after adding the saline solution to the preparation.
2. Explain the process that has occurred.
3. This experiment demonstrates that the plasma membrane is semi-permeable and the cell wall is permeable. Research the meaning of these terms. Then, think of a hypothesis to explain this demonstration.

Discovery techniques

OBSERVING CELLULAR FORMS IN INFUSIONS

> How can we cultivate microorganisms?

There are a whole host of microorganisms in our surroundings. They are everywhere: on the table, on our clothes, in the air we breathe, on our skin and inside our bodies.

AIMS

- Prepare a **growth medium** to cultivate microorganisms.
- Observe microorganisms using a microscope.

MATERIALS

- microscope
- beaker
- dropper or pipette
- slide
- coverslip
- field guides of unicellular organisms and invertebrates
- puddle water
- grasses, dry leaves and bits of vegetables

PROCEDURE

1. In a beaker, boil grasses, dry leaves and bits of vegetables for 15 minutes. Then leave the infusion to cool.

2. Collect water from a puddle or pond and add it to the infusion. Leave the mixture to rest in a well-lit place for a week.

3. Take a sample of the mixture with the dropper and place a drop on one of the slides. Place a coverslip over the top and observe it under a microscope.

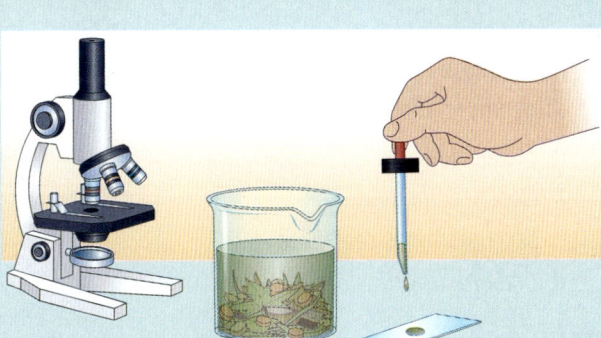

4. Repeat the observations, taking samples from different areas of the beaker: the surface, the bottom, next to a leaf, etc.

CONCLUSIONS

1. Describe and draw everything you can observe in your notebook.
2. Try to identify the microorganisms from your observations with the help of the field guides or the Internet.
3. Propose a hypothesis to explain the mechanisms that are used by the microorganisms you have observed to be able to move. Do they all move in the same way?

Revision activities

1. What is the difference between organic compounds and inorganic compounds? Which form part of living things?

2. Indicate which statements are incorrect and then correct them.
   a. Proteins are macromolecules made up of smaller molecules, called nucleotides, linking together to form a chain.
   b. Lipids are macromolecules made of a chain of carbon and hydrogen.
   c. Carbohydrates, also called monosaccharides, are the fuel for living things.
   d. Nucleic acids are small molecules made up of simpler molecules, called nucleotides, joining together.

3. Who observed living cells for the first time through a microscope, Robert Hooke or Anton van Leeuwenhoek? Explain why.

4. Search for information on the compound microscope. Then, copy the following diagram and label its main parts. Explain the function of each part.

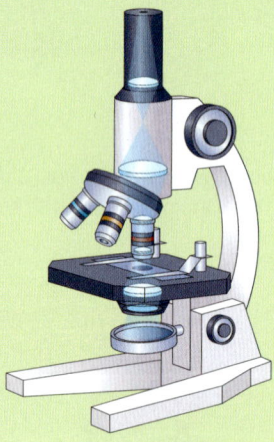

5. Together with your classmates, design a poster showing the basic principles of cell theory and the contributions of the different researchers.

6. Name and define the three basic components of any cell. What are their functions?

7. Which cells are older, eukaryotes or prokaryotes? Justify your answer.

8. What is a nucleoid? Name the group of organisms whose cells have nucleoids.

9. Explain Lynn Margulis' theory of endosymbiosis.

10. What is the main difference between prokaryotic and eukaryotic organisms?

11. Draw and label the structures of a bacterium.

12. The following diagrams are of a plant cell and an animal cell.
    a. Which diagram belongs to each cell? Justify your answer.
    b. Copy the following diagrams and label their main parts.

A

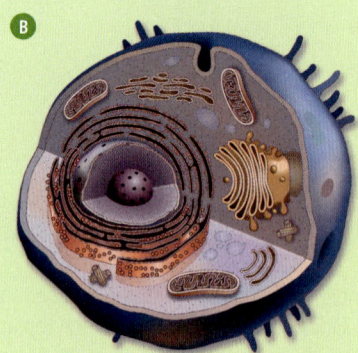

B

13. Research which cellular organisation model belongs to the following living things; search for images of them and some information on their lifestyle:
    a. *Escherichia coli*
    b. *Nostoc commune*
    c. *Saccharomyces cerevisiae*
    d. *Codium decorticatum*

14. List the structures and organelles of eukaryotic cells which do not appear in prokaryotic cells and vice versa.

15. Name three eukaryotic organisms that are unicellular and another three that are multicellular.

16. List the structures and organelles of plant cells which do not appear in animal cells and vice versa.

17. Indicate the organelles that appear in both animal and plant cells. Describe their functions.

18 Among the organelles and structures included in a plant cell and not in an animal cell are ...

   a. lysosomes and the centrosome.
   b. the cell wall and chloroplasts.
   c. vacuoles and mitochondria.
   d. the nucleus.

19 Indicate which of the following statements are true. Correct any which are false.

   a. Lignin accumulates in the cell membranes of animals to make them more fluid-like.
   b. In tissues, cells join up with each other because of substances which they secrete to make up the extracellular matrix.
   c. The cytosol is formed of three types of filaments: microfilaments, centrioles and intermediate filaments.
   d. Ribosomes comprise two subunits of proteins and DNA.
   e. The endoplasmic reticulum can be rough or smooth, depending on whether microtubules are present on their outer membrane or not.
   f. Photosynthesis (characteristic of plant cells) is carried out inside mitochondria.
   g. The diplosome is made up of two perpendicularly arranged structures called centrosomes.

20 Explain the main function of cholesterol in the plasma membrane of animal cells. What would happen if there were no cholesterol in the membrane?

21 The cell wall is a resistant and complex network present in plant cells. What is it made of?

22 Describe the centrosome of animal cells. What is their function in the cell?

23 Indicate whether the following statements are true or false and correct the false ones.

   a. Amoeboid movement is possible because of the coordinated activity of the nucleic fibres that make up the cytoskeleton.
   b. Amoeboid movement is typical of muscle cells.
   c. Amoeboid movement is typical of cells which have pili or flagella.
   d. All bacteria move by means of pili and cilia.

24 What do ribosomes consist of and what do they do? Where are they located? Are all ribosomes the same size?

25 Draw and label the rough and the smooth endoplasmic reticulum.

26 What is the Golgi body? What does it do?

27 What is the difference between anabolism and catabolism?

28 Decide whether cellular respiration is an anabolism or a catabolic process and explain why. What about photosynthesis?

29 Develop a theory explaining the type of reactions (catabolic or anabolic) that occur in muscle cells when doing physical activity.

30 Where does the energy used in anabolism come from?

31 In which cell organelles can DNA be found?

32 Do you think that photosynthetic organisms can use any type of electromagnetic radiation? Justify your answer.

33 What are the reagents in the photosynthesis equation? What about the products? Classify both reagents and products into organic and inorganic substances.

34 Outline the similarities and differences between the chemical equations which represent cellular respiration and photosynthesis.

35 What are thylakoids? Where are they located? What is their function?

36 Where do the processes of respiration and photosynthesis take place in cells? Are they catabolic or anabolic processes?

37 Which eukaryotic cell organelle is in charge of each of the following functions?

   a. Creation of organic material from inorganic material.
   b. Production of energy from glucose and oxygen.
   c. Elimination of toxic substances by oxidation reactions.
   d. Control and supervision of cell functioning.

38 Decide whether the following statement is true or false and explain why:
Plasmolysis is the contraction of a cell due to the loss of water through exocytosis.

Read and think

STEM CELLS: THE SECRET TO CHANGE

"Stem cells are a very special family of cells. When most other cells divide, the daughter cells look and act exactly like their parents. For example, a skin cell can't make anything but another skin cell. The same is true for cells in the intestine or liver. Not stem cells. Stem cells can become many different types. That is how an embryo grows from a single fertilised egg into a foetus with trillions of specialized cells. They need to specialise to make up tissues that function very differently, including those in the brain, skin, muscle and other organs. Later in life, stem cells can also replace worn-out or damaged cells.

Some stem cells can mature into any type of cell in the body. Such stem cells are called **pluripotent**. This word means 'having many possibilities'. And it's not hard to understand why these cells have captured the imaginations of many scientists.

At University of Nebraska Medical Center in Omaha, Iqbal Ahmad is a **neuroscientist** working on using stem cells to restore sight to people who lost it when nerve cells in the eye's retina died from a disease called **glaucoma**.

Located inside the back of the eye, the retina converts incoming light into electrical signals that are then sent to the brain. Ahmad is studying how to replace dead retina cells with new ones formed from pluripotent stem cells.

The neuroscientist starts by removing adult stem cells from the cornea, or the clear tissue that covers the front of the eye. These stem cells normally replace cells lost through the wear and tear of blinking. They cannot become nerve cells – at least not on their own. Ahmad, however, can transform these cornea stem cells into pluripotent stem cells. Then, with **prodding**, he turns them into nerve cells.

To make the transformation, Ahmad places the cornea cells on one side of a Petri dish. He then places stem cells on the other side. A **meshlike** membrane separates the two types of cells so they can't mix. But even though they can't touch, they do communicate.

Cells constantly send out chemical signals to which other cells respond. When the stem cells 'speak', the eye cells 'listen'. Their chemical messages persuade the eye cells to turn off the genes that tell them to be cornea cells. Over time, the eye cells become stem cells that can give rise to different types of cells, including nerve cells.

After transforming adult cornea stem cells from mice into nerve cells, Ahmad's team implanted the nerve cells into the eyes of laboratory mice and rats. Then, the cells migrated to the retina! There, they began replacing the nerve cells that had died from glaucoma. One day, the same procedure may **restore** vision to people who have lost their sight."

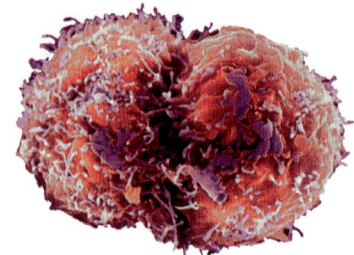

⬥ Mammalian stem cells

Adapted from *Science News for Students*, Society for Science & the Public

ANSWER THE QUESTIONS

1. In your own words, explain what a stem cell is.

2. Summarise the process that Ahmad's team follows to restore vision to mice with glaucoma.

3. It might be surprising to you, but plants also have stem cells! Hypothesise what the main differences between an animal and a plant stem cell might be.

4. Make a diagram of a mouse cornea stem cell. Make sure to draw and label all organelles. (Hint: think about what kind of cell it is: an eukaryote or a prokaryote? A plant or an animal cell?)

5. Why do you think it is necessary to place a meshlike membrane between cornea stem cells and pluripotent stem cells? If you can't think of any possible reasons, do some research online.

6. Investigations using stem cells are often a controversial issue. Do some research to find out why. Hold a debate in class. Your teacher will tell you whether you have to argue for or against the use of stem cells in research. To prepare your arguments, look for pieces of news talking about stem cell research and think about the associated implications.

Work it out

CONCEPT MAP

Use the words in the word cloud to create your own unit map in your notebook. Write any connecting texts you need.

vacuoles   mitochondria   lysosomes   nucleoid   plant cell
mesosomes   peroxisomes   bacterium cell
cell wall   **prokaryotic**   nucleus
cell organelles   **Cells**   plasma membrane   ribosomes
Golgi body
cytoplasm   **eukaryotic**   capsule   chloroplasts
animal cell   endoplasmic reticulum   centrosome
flagella

SELF-ASSESSMENT

Carry out a self-assessment of what you learned in this unit. Choose one answer for each question and then check your answers.

1 Living things are composed of ...
  a. inorganic compounds only.
  b. organic compounds only.
  c. both inorganic and organic compounds.

2 Who discovered the microbial world?
  a. Anton van Leeuwenhoek
  b. Santiago Ramón y Cajal
  c. Rudolf Virchow

3 Cells without a nuclear membrane are called ...
  a. symbiotic.
  b. eukaryotic.
  c. prokaryotic.

4 Most prokaryotic organisms are ...
  a. archaebacteria.
  b. cyanobacteria.
  c. eubacteria.

5 Which of these organelles is found only in animal cells?
  a. Centrosome
  b. Vacuole
  c. Ribosome

6 The plasma membrane of animal cells is made of ...
  a. lipids, cholesterol and nucleic acids.
  b. lipids, proteins and cholesterol.
  c. proteins, cholesterol and macromolecules.

7 Which of these is not a type of cytoskeleton filament?
  a. Intermediate tubules
  b. Microtubules
  c. Microfilaments

8 The organelles that contain RNA are ...
  a. ribosomes.
  b. centrosomes.
  c. lysosomes.

9 At mitochondria, respiration requires ...
  a. water and carbon dioxide.
  b. glucose and carbon dioxide.
  c. glucose and oxygen.

10 Which of the following is not found inside the nucleus?
  a. Nucleoli
  b. Endoplasmic reticulum
  c. Histones

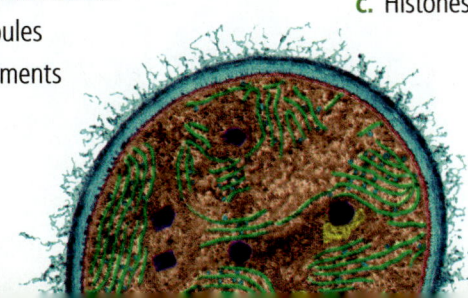

02 Cell reproduction

<<LOOKING BACK

- What way do the organisms in images A and C reproduce? Are these sexual or asexual modes of reproduction?
- Which way do animals reproduce, sexually or asexually? What about plants?
- What is the cell nucleus responsible for?
- What is the main function of nucleic acids?
- Image B shows the process of cell division in onion root cells. What do you think the red substance in them is?

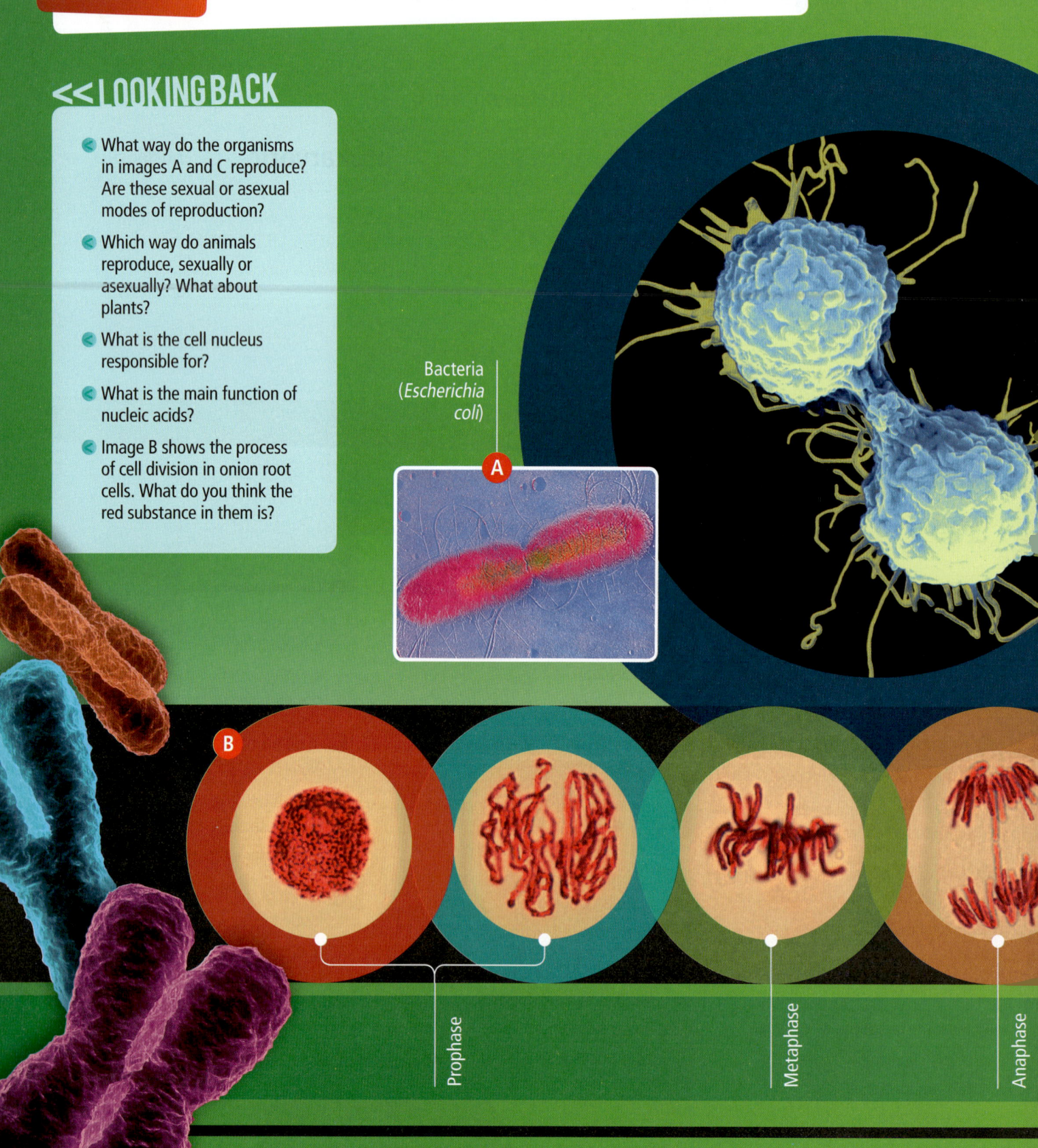

Bacteria (*Escherichia coli*)

Prophase · Metaphase · Anaphase

A very scientific pub

The Eagle pub in Cambridge, England, has a long and interesting history. It opened in 1667 during the era of the Great Fire of London and the Black Death, and during the Second World War, it was frequented by airmen stationed on the airfields around the city.

In 1953, *The Eagle* was a popular lunchtime destination for the staff of Cambridge University's nearby Cavendish Laboratory. One day in February, two scientists, J. Watson and F. Crick, walked in and announced that they had discovered 'the secret of life' – and nine years later they won the Nobel Prize for their work.

The world isn't changed only on battlefields or in business meetings. Scientific theories, literary arguments, even social revolutions have come into existence in ordinary public places such as pubs. Cambridge has produced over 80 Nobel Prize winners, and they probably all had a meal in this very pub – though not at the same time. That would be an extraordinary party!

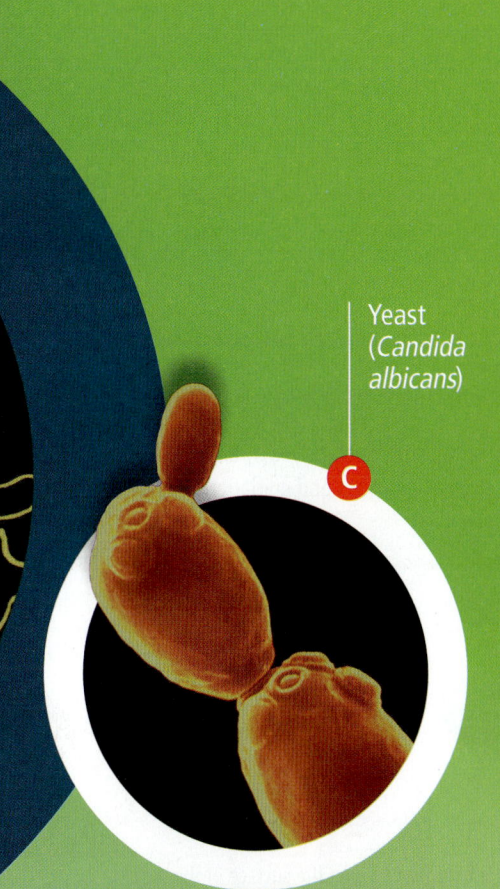

Yeast (*Candida albicans*)

- What do you think the 'secret of life' that Watson and Crick discovered was? Why did they call it that?
- Why was their breakthrough so important?
- What do you know about the other scientists who contributed to this discovery?

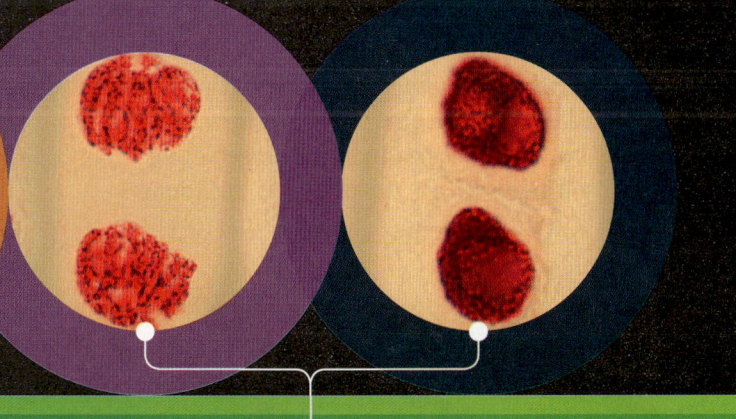

Telophase

LOOKING FORWARD >>

- What are the advantages of sexual reproduction?
- Why is DNA packaged in the form of chromosomes?
- What is the heterogametic sex in humans?
- What is mitosis?
- Why is meiosis important in sexual reproduction?
- What type of life cycle do humans have?
- How is a karyotype made?
- How can we observe cells in mitosis?

UNIT 02 Cell reproduction

1. The reproduction of living things

> What are the advantages of sexual reproduction?

Reproduction is the process by which living things produce new individuals of the same species. New living things can arise from individual cells, groups of cells or different parts of parent organisms.

In all cases, cells are the fundamental units from which the new living things develop.

- In **unicellular living things**, the cell is the whole organism. It divides to create new cells and, therefore, new organisms.
- In **multicellular living things**, the cells they are comprised of originate from others through a series of divisions. In the majority of cases, certain cells are specialised to perform the process of reproduction.

ASEXUAL REPRODUCTION

In **asexual reproduction**, a single parent produces new generations of individuals without the involvement of sex cells. There are various types of asexual reproduction.

BINARY FISSION

This occurs in unicellular organisms, such as protozoa and certain algae, and in multicellular organisms: this is how their cells and many tumours multiply.

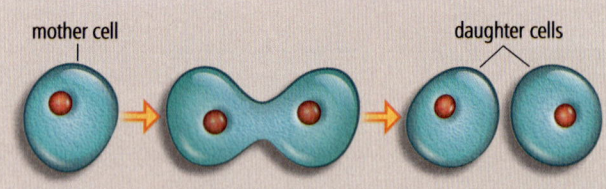

○ A cell, called the **mother cell**, first divides its nucleus and then its cytoplasm into two equally-sized daughter cells.

BUDDING

This occurs in unicellular organisms, such as yeast, and in multicellular organisms, such as sponges and cnidarians.

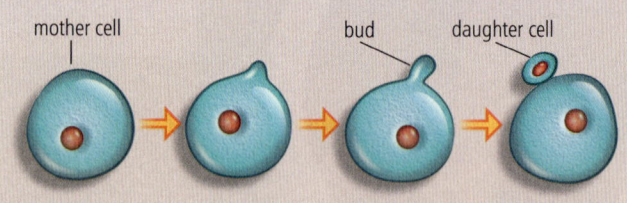

○ A protrusion, known as a **bud**, appears on the surface of the parent, and it is from this that a new individual is formed.

MULTIPLE FISSION

This is common in protozoa, and consists of the repeated division of the nucleus. One particular case is **sporulation**, in which the daughter cells, the **spores**, are surrounded by a protective casing that allows them to delay their development until the environmental conditions are suitable.

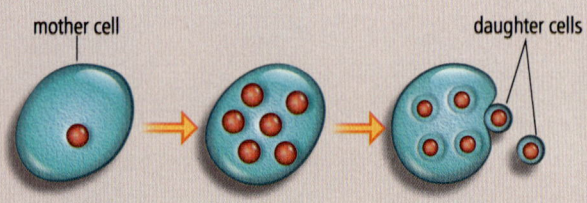

○ The numerous nuclei share out the cytoplasm and the plasma membrane, forming small daughter cells that are released when the mother cell ruptures.

FRAGMENTATION

This type of reproduction is common in some animals like starfish and planaria. In plants there are many different types of reproduction by fragmentation; some examples are **rhizomes** (fern), **bulbs** (onion), **tubers** (potato) and **runners** (strawberry).

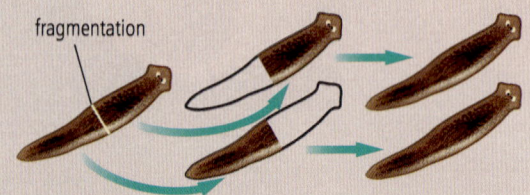

○ Fragmentation is the process by which a multicellular organism divides into two or more segments. Each of these segments can give rise to a whole organism.

SEXUAL REPRODUCTION

This form of reproduction involves two parents who produce specialised cells: **gametes**. The majority of the species are **single-sexed** or **dioecious**. This means that individuals of different sexes (male and female) generate the gametes. It can happen that the two types of gametes come from a single individual, known as a **hermaphrodite** or **monoecious species**. In both cases, the fusion of two compatible gametes will produce new individuals.

Sexual reproduction involves a series of different processes:

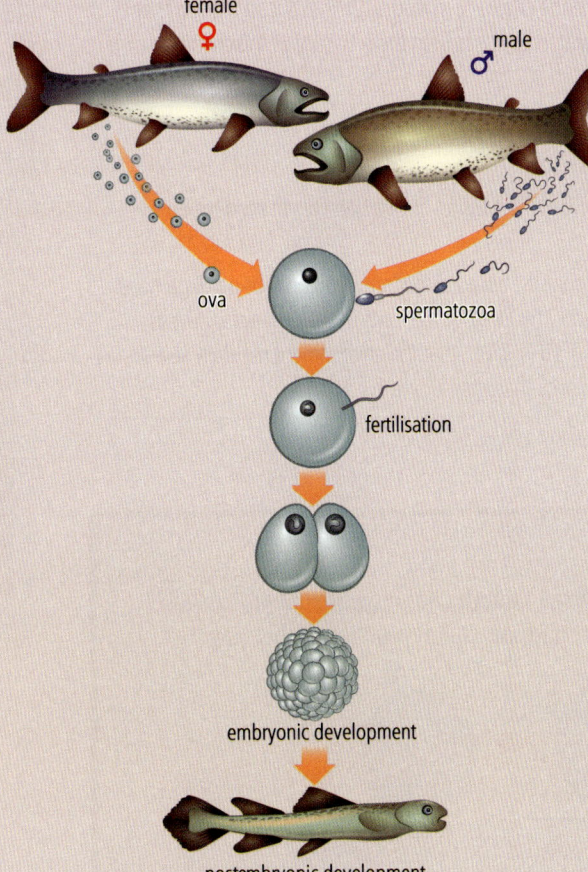

1 Gametogenesis. This is the formation of male and female gametes. In animals, the masculine gametes are the **spermatozoa** and the female are the **ova**; in plants, they are **antherozoids** and **oospheres**, respectively.

2 Fertilisation. This is the fusion of the male and female gametes to form the new cell, called **fertilised egg** or **zygote**.

3 Embryonic development. This includes cell divisions of the zygote to form an **embryo** and its maturation until the moment of its birth (in animals), or until seed formation (in plants).

4 Postembryonic development. This is the process which, after birth or germination, culminates in the formation of an adult with the ability to reproduce.

ACTIVITIES

1. Is it correct to say that living things originate from individual cells? Explain your answer.

2. In your own words, briefly explain the following terms: *gametogenesis*, *fertilisation*, *embryonic development* and *postembryonic development*.

3. State the difference between reproduction in unicellular organisms and reproduction in multicellular organisms.

4. Is it correct to associate asexual reproduction with unicellular organisms and sexual reproduction with multicellular organisms? Explain your answer.

5. A new plant can sometimes be obtained from part of another plant. Is this a type of reproduction? Which type of reproduction would you include this in?

UNIT 02 Cell reproduction

1.1 Advantages and disadvantages of asexual and sexual reproduction

ASEXUAL REPRODUCTION
- This is simpler than sexual reproduction.
- It guarantees rapid and effective growth of populations with the involvement of a single original individual.
- Its main **drawback** is that offspring possess genetic material that is practically identical to that of their parents. As a result, the characteristics of all the individuals of a population are the same. This means that a hostile environmental change can lead to their extinction, given that there are no individuals with different characteristics allowing them to survive the change.

SEXUAL REPRODUCTION
- This is more complex than asexual reproduction.
- It requires both a female and male, and involves the fusion of two gametes to produce an offspring.
- It occurs in the majority of multicellular organisms because the formation and fusion of gametes causes variety in the hereditary material and, therefore, in the traits of the organisms. This is an advantage from an evolutionary point of view, given that the environment naturally selects individuals from each population with the best characteristics to live in it.

> ### HERMAPHRODITISM
> There are species in which an individual has male and female reproductive organs. Although in animals the term *hermaphrodite* is synonymous with *monoecious*, when talking about plants, the word *monoecius* is more often used to refer to species which (like pine trees) have separate male and female flowers on the same plant. The word *hermaphrodite*, on the other hand, is used for plants with stamens and pistils in the same flower.
>
> Hermaphroditism does not mean **self-fertilising**. Fertilisation is almost always crossed; as such, it contributes to the main objective of sexual reproduction: to create a variety of genetic material.
>
>
>
> ◦ Self-fertilisation in hermaphroditic snails is possible but rare.

ACTIVITIES

6. The diagram represents a type of cell reproduction. Is it sexual or asexual? What is it called? Name various organisms that reproduce in this way.

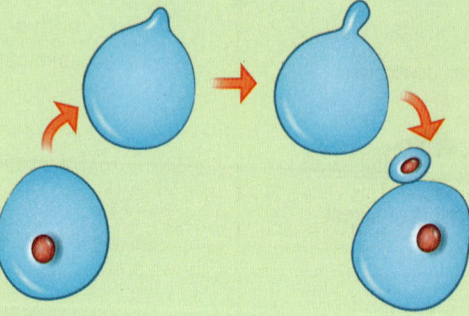

7. Which species would be more vulnerable to a parasitic infection, one that reproduces sexually or asexually? Justify your answer

8. Why does sexual reproduction occur in the majority of organisms, despite being more complex than asexual reproduction?

9. What are the advantages of a certain species being able to reproduce sexually and asexually?

10. Explain why hermaphroditic organisms do not usually self-fertilise.

11. Decide whether the following statement is true or false and explain why:
    The main evolutionary advantage of sexual reproduction is the increase in variation in the hereditary material. This involves a rapid population growth.

12. Develop a theory on the biological significance of hermaphroditism for a species.

2. The cell cycle

> Why is DNA packaged in the form of chromosomes?

Organisms use cell division in reproduction, development and growth processes. This division alternates with periods in which the cell does not divide, although it is preparing itself for **potential** future divisions. In certain cases, the cell never divides, but specialises in a certain function until it dies.

The **cell cycle** is the sequence of events that occur from the moment a cell is formed until it divides and creates new cells.

The cell cycle of eukaryotic cells comprises two phases: **M phase** or **division phase** and **interphase**.

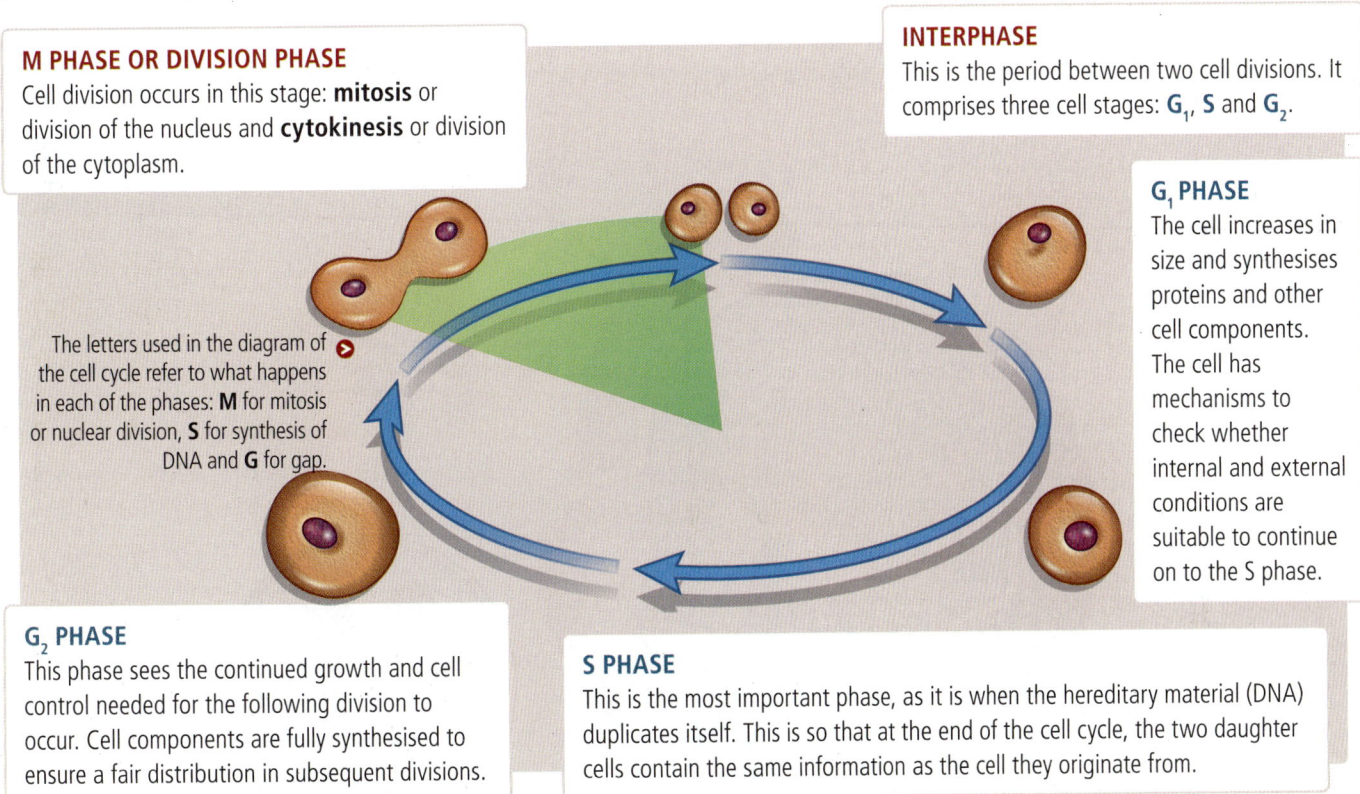

M PHASE OR DIVISION PHASE
Cell division occurs in this stage: **mitosis** or division of the nucleus and **cytokinesis** or division of the cytoplasm.

> The letters used in the diagram of the cell cycle refer to what happens in each of the phases: **M** for mitosis or nuclear division, **S** for synthesis of DNA and **G** for gap.

INTERPHASE
This is the period between two cell divisions. It comprises three cell stages: G_1, S and G_2.

G_1 PHASE
The cell increases in size and synthesises proteins and other cell components. The cell has mechanisms to check whether internal and external conditions are suitable to continue on to the S phase.

G_2 PHASE
This phase sees the continued growth and cell control needed for the following division to occur. Cell components are fully synthesised to ensure a fair distribution in subsequent divisions.

S PHASE
This is the most important phase, as it is when the hereditary material (DNA) duplicates itself. This is so that at the end of the cell cycle, the two daughter cells contain the same information as the cell they originate from.

The **duration of the cell cycle** of a mammal cell varies greatly. In **cell cultures**, a complete cycle lasts 23 hours, with interphase lasting 22 hours and M phase less than an hour. The S phase takes between 10 and 12 hours and the rest is shared between the G_1 and G_2 phases.

> When conditions outside the cell are not favourable, the G_1 phase is longer, occasionally lasting for months or even years. When this happens, it is called the G_0 phase. Many cells, like neurones, remain in this state until the cells themselves (or the organism they belong to) die.

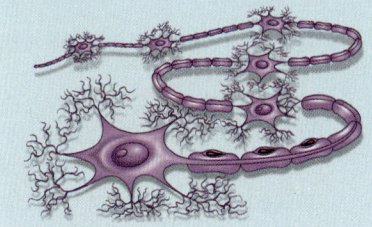

◭ Neurons

ACTIVITIES

13. In which life processes are cell divisions most frequent?

14. Explain the importance of the S phase of the cell cycle.

15. Some researchers are cultivating mammal cells whose complete cell cycle usually lasts between 22 and 23 hours. In one of the cultures, it is confirmed at the end of this time period that the cell concentration is the same, or in other words, it has not completed its cell cycle. What does this mean? Develop a hypothesis that attempts to explain what has happened.

2.1 The nucleus in interphase

Interphase is an intensively active stage of the cell cycle. In addition to the expression of genetic material, **DNA is duplicated** during the S phase. This replication is needed for the daughter cells to receive an identical share of the genetic material.

The components of the nucleus that can be observed during interphase are the nuclear lamina, nucleoli, the nuclear membrane, the nucleoplasm and chromatin.

> ### THE SHAPE OF THE NUCLEUS
> The shape of the nucleus can be very varied, although it is usually spherical or ovoid. Spherical-shaped nuclei are common in animal cells and are usually located in the middle of the cell. Ovoid nuclei are typical of plant cells and are usually displaced from the centre of the cell by the pressure of large vacuoles.

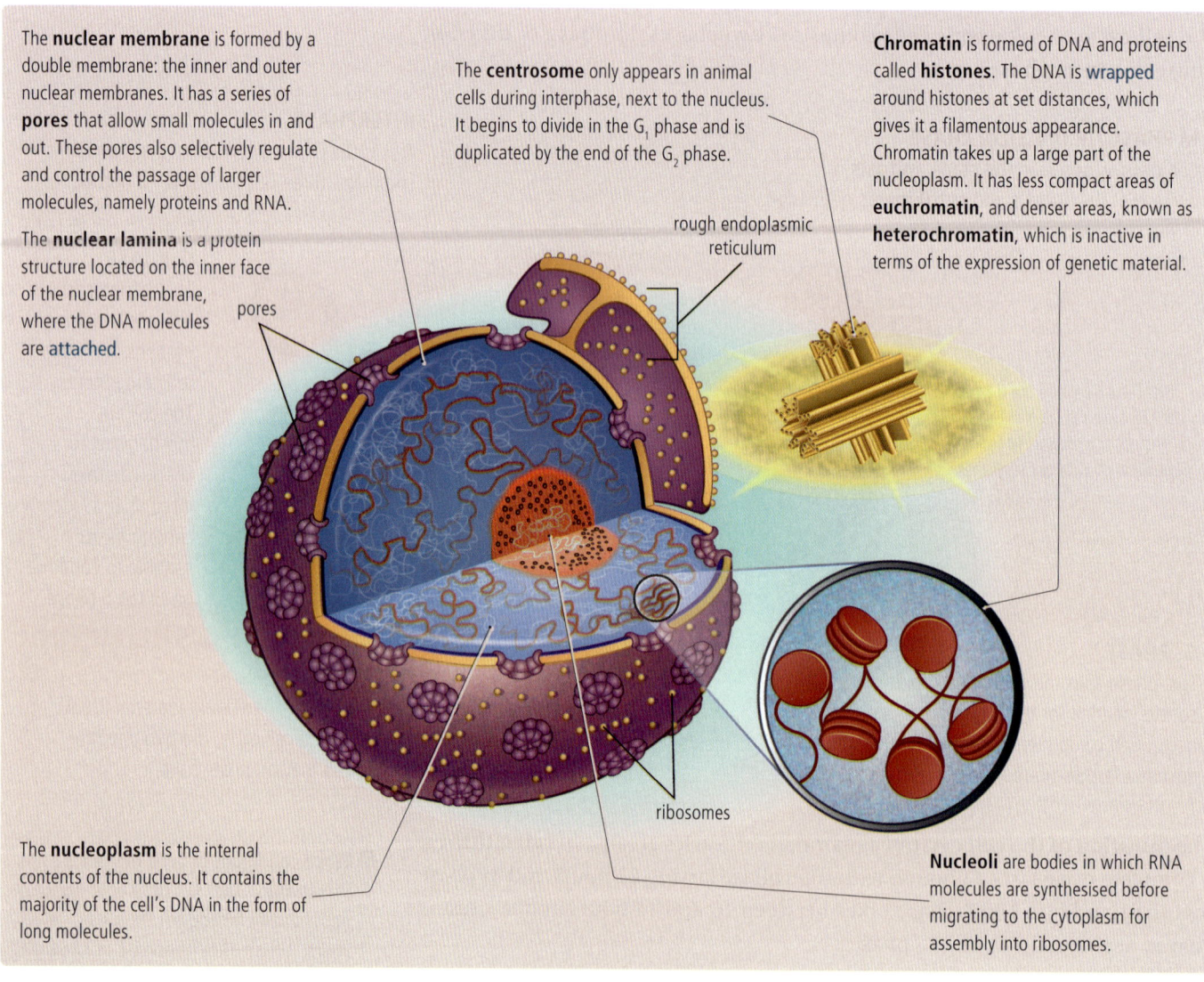

The **nuclear membrane** is formed by a double membrane: the inner and outer nuclear membranes. It has a series of **pores** that allow small molecules in and out. These pores also selectively regulate and control the passage of larger molecules, namely proteins and RNA.

The **nuclear lamina** is a protein structure located on the inner face of the nuclear membrane, where the DNA molecules are **attached**.

The **centrosome** only appears in animal cells during interphase, next to the nucleus. It begins to divide in the G_1 phase and is duplicated by the end of the G_2 phase.

Chromatin is formed of DNA and proteins called **histones**. The DNA is **wrapped** around histones at set distances, which gives it a filamentous appearance. Chromatin takes up a large part of the nucleoplasm. It has less compact areas of **euchromatin**, and denser areas, known as **heterochromatin**, which is inactive in terms of the expression of genetic material.

The **nucleoplasm** is the internal contents of the nucleus. It contains the majority of the cell's DNA in the form of long molecules.

Nucleoli are bodies in which RNA molecules are synthesised before migrating to the cytoplasm for assembly into ribosomes.

ACTIVITIES

16. What is the relationship between the terms nucleoplasm and cytoplasm?

17. The nuclear lamina is a protein structure located on the inner face of the nuclear membrane. DNA molecules are attached to the inside of it by their ends. Develop various hypotheses which attempt to explain the possible function of this attachment.

18. Red blood cells in almost all mammals do not have a nucleus. Look for information and find out why the loss of the nucleus is considered an evolutionary advantage. Which other cell components do erythrocytes lack?

19. Which type of cell is the centrosome found in? What is its function?

2.2 The nucleus in division: chromosomes

When the cell starts to divide, the nucleus changes in appearance:

- The nuclear lamina and the nucleoli disappear and the nuclear membrane breaks down.
- The nucleoplasm is released into the cytosol and the nuclear contents are distributed throughout the cytoplasm.
- The chromatin fibres slowly coil themselves up to form a DNA package approximateley 10 000 times shorter than the linear DNA free of proteins. In this way, they are visible under an optical microscope as **rod-shaped** bodies called **chromosomes**.

DNA PACKAGING

The packaging of genetic material serves two functions:

- On the one hand, the sister DNA molecules **tangled up** in the nucleoplasm (originating from the duplication in the S phase) line up next to each other. This facilitates their subsequent separation.
- On the other hand, the large DNA molecules are made more resistant to breakage during cell division as they are packaged into chromosomes.

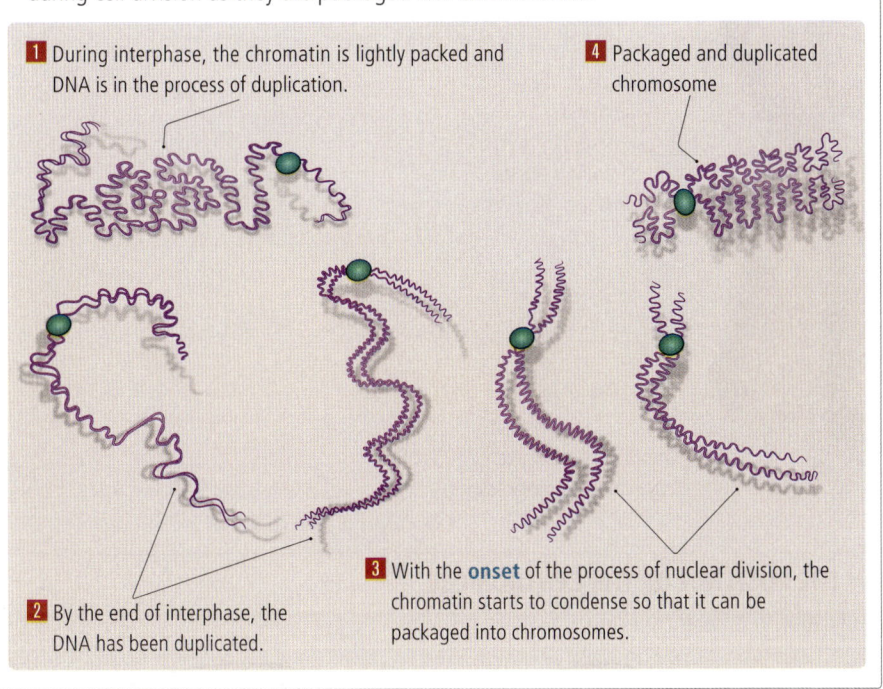

1 During interphase, the chromatin is lightly packed and DNA is in the process of duplication.

4 Packaged and duplicated chromosome

2 By the end of interphase, the DNA has been duplicated.

3 With the **onset** of the process of nuclear division, the chromatin starts to condense so that it can be packaged into chromosomes.

ACTIVITIES

20. Make a labelled drawing that shows the differences between a dividing cell nucleus and another in interphase.
21. What do you think would happen if DNA were not packaged in the form of chromosomes?
22. Look for information on Rosalind Franklin and Watson and Crick's discovery and write a short report about their biographies and their contribution to science.

BIG THINKER

Rosalind Franklin was an exceptionally intelligent child, so it was unsurprising that she would become a brilliant scientist – but it would be a challenging choice. She graduated from Cambridge University in 1941 but **wasn't awarded** her degree for six years because women were prohibited from receiving them! Franklin was the first to hypothesise the double-helix DNA molecule, and even showed it existed through X-ray **diffraction**, yet her work was used by Watson and Crick as the basis for their DNA model, and they took all the credit! If someone became famous for your discovery, what would you do?

DID YOU KNOW?

The **average** diameter of the nucleus of a human cell is approximately 6 μm (6×10^{-6} m). If all the DNA molecules contained in a nucleus were joined end-to-end, without condensation or packaging, they would measure approximately 2 m in length.
Geometrically, this situation is comparable to introducing a 15 km-long thread into a chicken egg. How could this be possible?

3 Chromosomes

> What is the heterogametic sex in humans?

Chromosomes are molecules of DNA joined to proteins which arise from the condensation and packaging of chromatin. Histones and other proteins help chromosomes condense and hold their structure.

3.1 Shape and size of chromosomes

Chromosomes vary in size and shape because of the changes they undergo throughout the cell cycle. They go from being lightly packed in interphase to being compact during mitosis.

Measurements of chromosome size are usually made during mitosis, when they appear more compact. Even so, the values for their size are relative, as they also depend on the technique and treatment used to fix and observe them under the microscope.

> Most **monocotyledonous plants**, amphibians and **orthopteran insects** have relatively large chromosomes of between 10 μm and 30 μm. The rest of the animals, algae, fungi and dicotyledonous plants have smaller chromosomes of less than 5 μm.

Each half of a chromosome is called a **chromatid**. Chromatids are identical DNA molecules that arise from the duplication in interphase and, for this reason, are known as **sister chromatids**.

At the end of the cell division, the sister chromatids are separated, so that each daughter cell receives a set of daughter chromosomes with just a chromatid each.

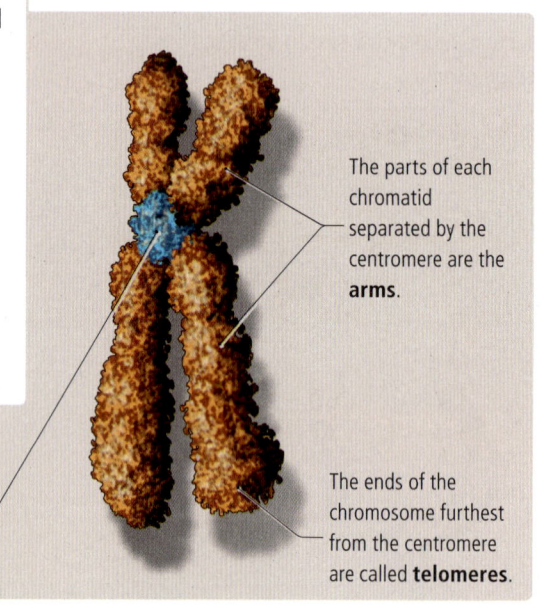

At the start of division, chromosomes appear as double strands joined by a constricted region, the **centromere**.

The parts of each chromatid separated by the centromere are the **arms**.

The ends of the chromosome furthest from the centromere are called **telomeres**.

TYPES OF CHROMOSOMES DEPENDING ON THE POSITION OF THE CENTROMERE
This classification is very useful as it aids their identification in different species.

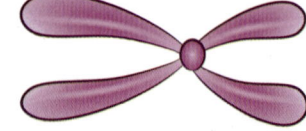

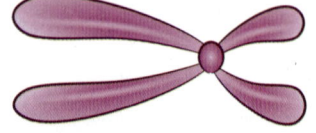

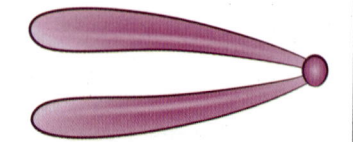

- **Metacentric**. The centromere is in the middle of the chromosome and the arms are of the same length.
- **Submetacentric**. The centromere is slightly off-centre and, as a result, the arms are unequal in length.
- **Acrocentric**. The centromere is close to one of the ends and the arms are very unequal in length.
- **Telocentric**. The centromere is at one end of the chromosome and, therefore, some arms hardly exist at all.

ACTIVITIES

23. Are chromosomal arms and chromatids the same thing? Justify your answer.

24. Why may the position of the centromere on the chromosomes be important to a biologist?

3.2 Sex chromosomes

In many organisms, one of the sexes has a pair of chromosomes that are different from each other. The chromosomes of this pair are called **heterochromosomes** or s**ex chromosomes**; the rest are called **autosomes**.

- In mammals, many insects and some plants, the male has an **X chromosome** and another smaller one, called the **Y chromosome**. Therefore, males are the **heterogametic** sex (X, Y). The females are **homogametic** (X, X) as their sex chromosomes are the same.
- In birds, reptiles and certain amphibians, the females (heterogametic sex) have two different sex chromosomes (W, Z), while the males (homogametic sex) have two of the same sex chromosomes (W, W).
- The Y chromosome does not exist for grasshoppers. The females have two X chromosomes while the males have just one. The males are said to be (X, zero) or (X, 0).

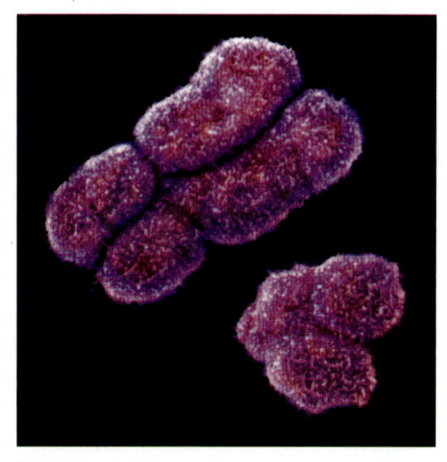

◯ Male human sex chromosomes (pair 23): X (left) and Y (right)

3.3 Number of chromosomes

The number of chromosomes in a species is not related to its amount of DNA or its complexity. There is also no direct connection between this number and the evolutive relationships of the species with other living things.

◯ The deer *Muntiacus reevesi* (left) has 2n = 46 chromosomes (same amount as the human species *Homo sapiens*) while the deer *Muntiacus muntjak* (right) has only 2n = 6 chromosomes.

Most eukaryotic organisms have two sets of chromosomes in their cells. The amount of chromosomes that each parent provides in their sex cells is the **haploid number** (represented as **n**). One set comes from the father and the other set from the mother. The total number of chromosomes is called the **diploid number** (represented as **2n**). This number is fixed and constant for every species, although it is very variable when comparing some species with others.

Somatic cells are those which are not involved in reproduction but make up organs and tissues of multicellular organisms; they contain two series or sets of chromosomes and, therefore, are diploid. They are different from **germ cells**, which are involved in reproduction and produce the gametes; these contain only one set of chromosomes and, therefore, are haploid.

In diploid cells, similar-looking chromosomes form pairs; each paired chromosome comes from a different parent. These pairs are called **homologous chromosomes**. They are almost identical DNA molecules which contain the hereditary information for the same morphological and functional features of an organism. The slight differences presented by each chromosome of the pair are what make each feature slightly different from one individual to another.

ACTIVITIES

25. Explain the following statement.

    In birds, the heterogametic sex is the female.

26. Which species has more chromosomes, a mammal or a plant? Explain your answer.

27. Can homologous chromosomes exist in a haploid cell? Explain your answer.

28. Can the diploid cells of a species have an odd number of chromosomes? Why?

29. Search for information on animal species in which the determination of sex does not depend on sex chromosomes.

3.4 Karyotypes

A **karyotype** is the complete set of pairs of chromosomes of a cell, classified and organised according to their shape and size.

Although all chromosomes share the same basic structure, they do have individual properties that allow them to be identified, compared and classified. These include their length, the position of the centromere and the presence of a characteristic banding pattern when stained.

HUMAN KARYOTYPES

Human cells normally contain 23 pairs of chromosomes (46 chromosomes in total). They are numbered 1–23 from top left to bottom right, the last pair being the sex chromosomes. Each member of a homologous pair is similar in length and banding pattern.

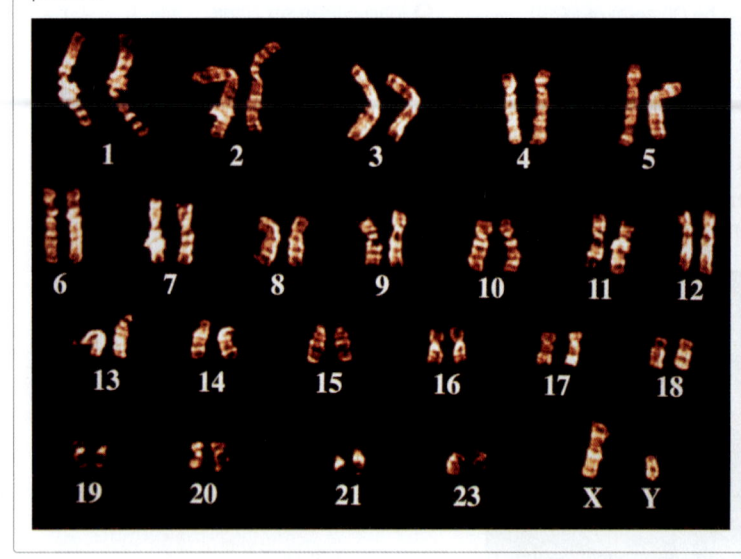

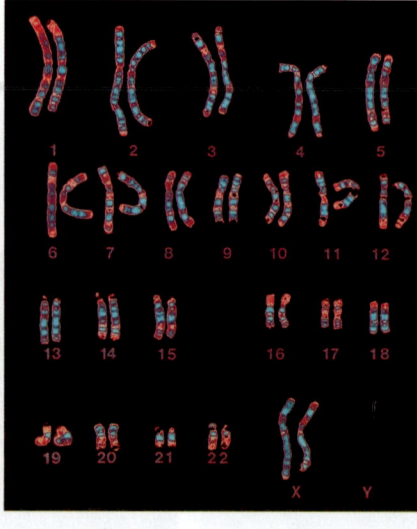

◀ Normal male (left) and female (right) human karotypes. Male and female sets differ only in the sex chromosomes: a male is labelled XY, a female XX.

One of the chromosome-staining methods that creates the typical banding patterns is the **Giemsa method**. For this reason, the bands that **stain** more darkly are called **G-bands**. The staining of some areas, compared with others that do not stain, is related to the different chemical composition of each specific area of DNA. Some areas retain the dye while others do not. Homologous chromosomes usually display the same pattern. This allows pairs of homologous chromosomes to be identified by the arrangement of their bands as well as by their size.

Karyotype analysis is done on cells when they are dividing so that the chromosomes are clearly visible under the microscope. **Micrographs** are taken of cell preparations and are **subsequently** cut up and re-organised.

▶ By comparing the karyotype of different individuals, changes can be observed in the banding pattern, which allows the detection of losses of chromosomal parts; movement of segments from some chromosomes to others; and even the appearance of three copies of a chromosome (trisomy). These visible alterations in the karyotype can be **linked** to certain types of cancer and other genetic abnormalities.

ACTIVITIES

30. Staining chromosomes with Giemsa usually produces the typical light and dark banding patterns. What is this useful for?

31. Look carefully at the karyotypes of a man and a woman above and state their differences.

32. In humans, the pairs of chromosomes 8 and 9 are very similar in size and the position of the centromere. What would you look at in order to distinguish them from each other?

33. Briefly explain what a karyotype is.

4. Cell division

> What is mitosis?

Cell division occurs in all cells, in both unicellular and multicellular organisms, after the genetic material has been duplicated in interphase. Firstly, the division of the nucleus or **mitosis** takes place, and then, almost always coinciding with the last phase of mitosis, the division of the cytoplasm or **cytokinesis** occurs.

MITOSIS

This is the division of the nucleus in eukaryotic cells. It involves the condensation of DNA into chromosomes and the separation of duplicated chromosomes to form two identical sets.

Although mitosis is a continuous process, for the purposes of explanation, it can be divided into four phases: prophase, metaphase, anaphase and telophase.

PROPHASE
Prophase starts with the condensation of chromatin in the nucleus, which forms **chromosomes** with their two sister chromatids joined together. Outside of the nucleus, the **mitotic spindle** starts to form. This is made up of protein fibres (microtubules) such as those from the cytoskeleton and the aster of the centrosome. In animal cells, the centrosomes, duplicated in interphase, are located at opposite poles of the spindle.

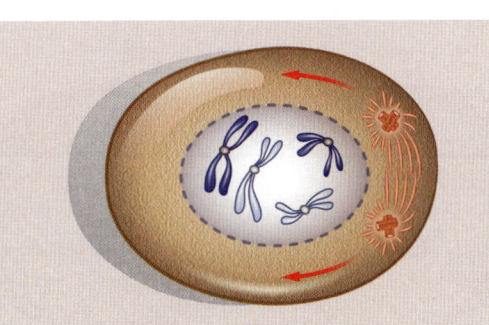

METAPHASE
The mitotic spindle lengthens. The completely-condensed chromosomes line up on the equator of the cell, which is perpendicular to the spindle. The microtubules joined to the centromere pull the sister chromatids towards the poles.

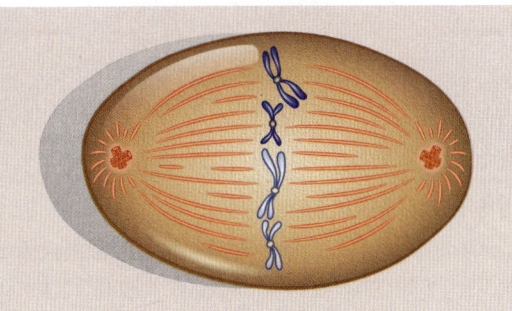

ANAPHASE
The sister chromatids separate and become **daughter chromosomes**, which are transported slowly to opposite ends of the mother cell.

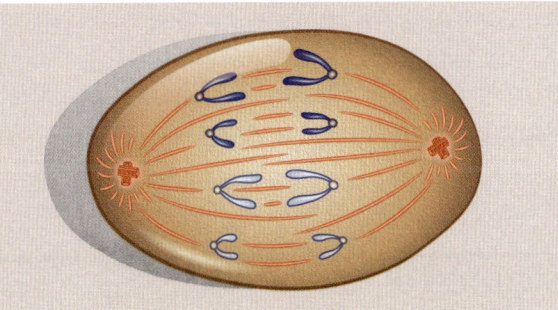

TELOPHASE
The new chromosomes reach the poles of the cell and start to **uncoil**, reverting back to their chromatin state. The new nuclear membrane appears around each set of daughter chromosomes. The end of telophase brings about the formation of the new nuclei and the appearance of the nucleoli. In animal cells, the respective centrosomes remain next to each nucleus.

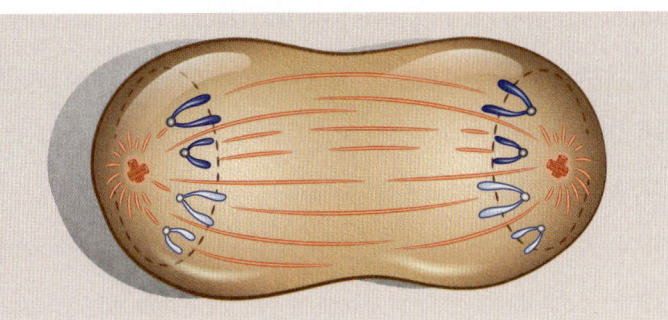

CYTOKINESIS

Once the nucleus is divided, the cytoplasm divides in telophase, with the corresponding distribution of the organelles. Cytokinesis occurs differently in animals and plants.

CYTOKINESIS IN ANIMAL CELLS

A ring of protein filaments, called the **contractile ring**, forms around the equator of the cell just underneath the plasma membrane. The contractile ring shrinks at the equator of the cell, **pinching** the plasma membrane inward, and forming what is called a **cleavage furrow**. Eventually, the contractile ring shrinks to the point that there are two separate daughter cells each surrounded by its own plasma membrane.

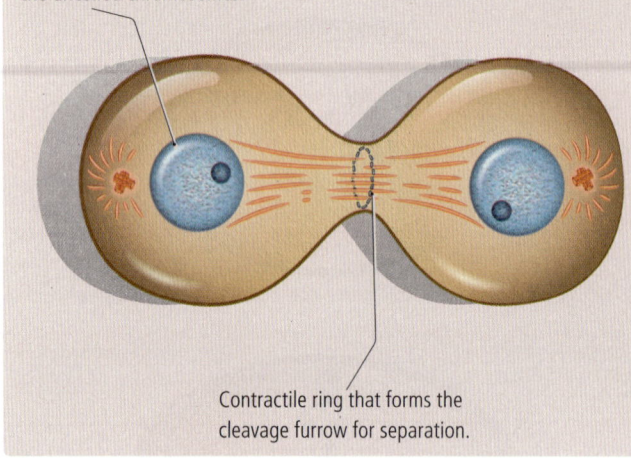

Complete nuclear membrane which surrounds the uncoiled chromosomes.

Contractile ring that forms the cleavage furrow for separation.

CYTOKINESIS IN PLANT CELLS

Because of the cell wall, cytokinesis is different in plant cells than it is in animal cells. **Vesicles** from the Golgi body assemble at the equatorial plane with the components that will form the cell wall. The vesicles join up with the microtubules of the spindle and fuse together. The membranes of the vesicles will make up the new cell membranes, and their contents will make up the cell wall.

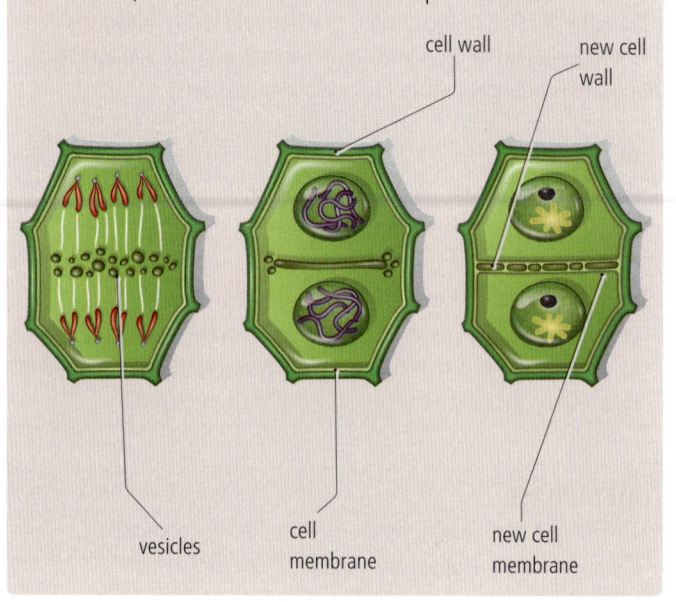

cell wall — new cell wall

vesicles — cell membrane — new cell membrane

CELL DIVISION IN PROKARYOTES

Bacteria's only molecule of circular DNA is attached to the cell membrane. In these organisms, the genetic material does not alter in length or thickness by condensation, unlike in eukaryotes.

When the cell is going to divide, the DNA duplicates itself to ensure that the two daughter cells have the same genetic information as the mother cell. The attachment sites of the daughter chromosomes on the nuclear membrane are on opposite poles of the cell. The plasma membrane and the cell wall reach all the way in at the equator, dividing the cell in two.

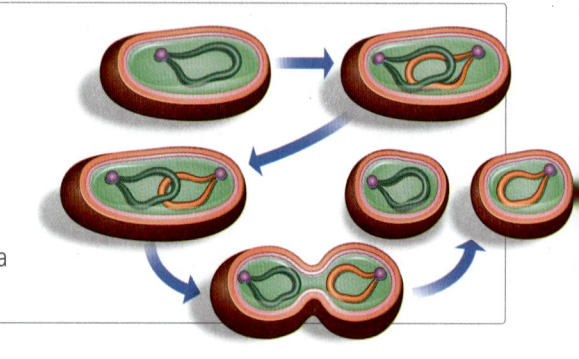

ACTIVITIES

34. Explain why chromosomes have two chromatids in prophase.
35. How many chromatids do chromosomes have in telophase? Why?
36. Does mitosis occur in prokaryotic cells? Explain your answer.
37. Is mitosis the same as cytokinesis? Explain why.
38. Draw and label the mitotic phases of a cell with four chromosomes.
39. Find out the etymological meaning of the terms used to name the four phases of mitosis.

5. The sexual reproduction cycle

> Why is meiosis important in sexual reproduction?

Sexual reproduction occurs in a cycle in which generations of haploid cells (n) are alternated with generations of diploid cells (2n).

The majority of the cells of multicellular organisms are diploid. However, in order to reproduce and maintain the right number of chromosomes for the species, the sex cells or gametes must be haploid cells. Meiosis is a special type of cell division in which haploid cells are created from diploid cells.

When both haploid gametes fuse together, they will create a diploid cell (an egg) which, through successive mitoses, will produce a new multicellular and diploid adult.

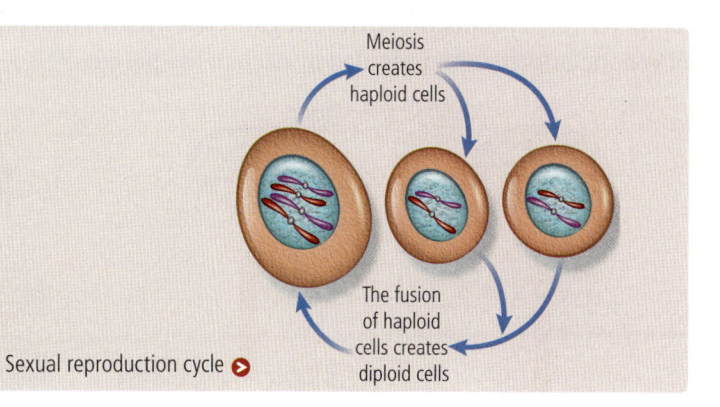

Sexual reproduction cycle

Meiosis creates haploid cells

The fusion of haploid cells creates diploid cells

5.1 Meiosis, a different type of cell division

Meiosis consists of two consecutive cell divisions (**first** and **second meiotic divisions**), each with four phases. It begins with a single **diploid mother cell** (2n) and produces **four haploid daughter cells** (n). Prior to the first division, the DNA is duplicated.

FIRST MEIOTIC DIVISION

PROPHASE I
The nuclear membrane starts to disperse and the spindle forms in the cytoplasm. The chromosomes, each with two chromatids, attach strongly to their homologous partners while condensing at the same time. It is during this pairing up when the exchange of genetic material between homologous chromosomes occurs. This process is known as **crossing over**.

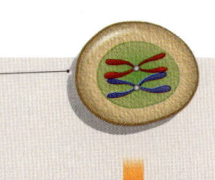

METAPHASE I
The nucleus can no longer be seen and the **pairs of homologous chromosomes** line up along the equator of the cell.

ANAPHASE I
The two members of each pair of homologous chromosomes **separate** and the microtubules from the spindle drag them towards opposite poles.

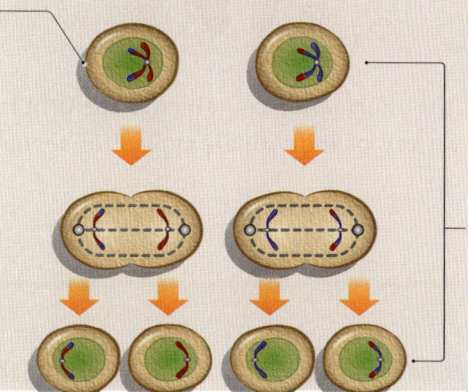

TELOPHASE I
The two new nuclei are located at each pole and chromatin is less condensed. In some cases, the nuclear membrane reforms. Each nucleus has a **haploid** number of duplicated chromosomes with **two chromatids**.

After this, the cytoplasm divides and there is an almost imperceptible interphase in which there is no DNA duplication.

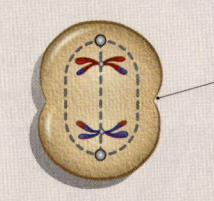

SECOND MEIOTIC DIVISION
This second division of the two haploid cells resulting from the first division follows a dynamic similar to mitosis: the sister chromatids of each chromosome separate. By the end of meiosis, there are **four haploid cells** with half the number of chromosomes as the mother cell.

5.2 The importance of meiosis in sexual reproduction

Meiosis is a process which maintains the **number of chromosomes** in a species with sexual reproduction. As this number of chromosomes is halved, it prevents them from doubling with each fertilisation over the generations. Homologous chromosomes are also distributed **randomly** between the daughter cells, producing **different gametes** with an independent assortment of genetic information provided by each of the parents.

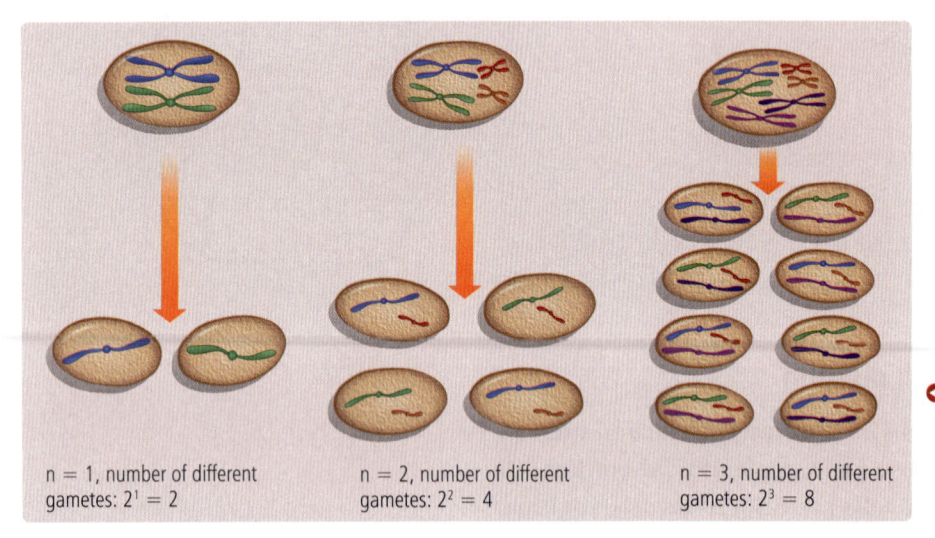

n = 1, number of different gametes: $2^1 = 2$

n = 2, number of different gametes: $2^2 = 4$

n = 3, number of different gametes: $2^3 = 8$

◁ During the first meiotic division, the homologous chromosomes from the mother and the father are distributed randomly. As a result, the number of different gametes that can arise depends on the number of pairs (n) of the species.

The number of different gametes that can be generated is 2^n, where *n* is the haploid number of chromosomes. The human species has the ability to produce, simply through the independent **assortment** of the 23 pairs of chromosomes, $2^{23} = 8\,388\,608$ different gametes.

The crossing over of chromosomes in prophase I causes DNA segments to be exchanged. As a result, when the maternal and paternal chromosomes from each homologous pair separate in anaphase I, some maternal chromatids have parts of paternal chromatids and vice-versa.

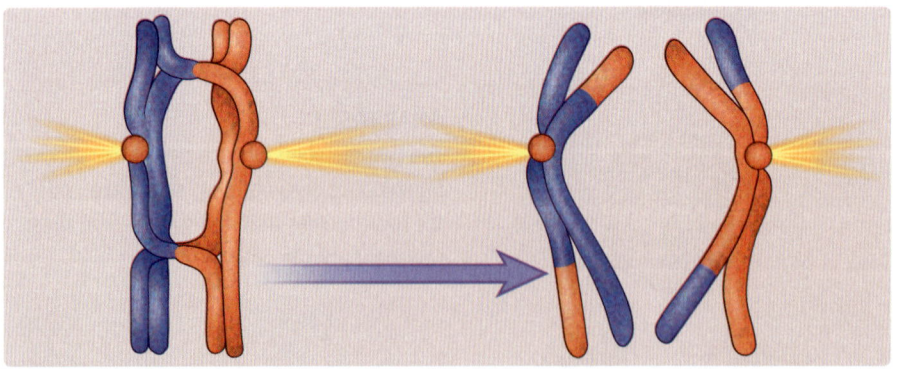

◁ Crossing over between non-sister cromatids. The homologous cromatids separate and exchange different segments of their genetic material to form **recombinant** chromosomes.

These meiotic occurrences recombine the information contained in the DNA in offspring. This results in the great variety of individuals typical of sexual reproduction.

ACTIVITIES

40. Why must gametes be haploid in sexual reproduction?

41. What does the number of different gametes that can be formed in sexual reproduction depend on?

5.3 Comparison between mitosis and meiosis

The main similarities and differences between the two processes are shown in the following table.

	MITOSIS	MEIOSIS
similarities	Both require the prior duplication of DNA.	
	The relative position of chromosomes is similar in equivalent phases.	
differences	Produces two daughter cells identical to the mother cell.	Produces four daughter cells that are genetically different from each other and the mother cell.
	The number of chromosomes is the same.	The number of chromosomes is halved.
	Involved in asexual reproduction, cell reproduction and tissue growth.	Involved in formation of gametes for sexual reproduction.

DID YOU KNOW?

There are about 64 trillion different offspring that can be created by a man and a woman. This means that if they had 64 trillion babies, there would never be two identical babies, unless they were identical twins. This variety is because of the crossing over of chromosomes in prophase I.

Identical twins (monozygotic twins) are mostly identical genetically. This is because they result from one zygote splitting into two or more separate ones within a few days after conception. Any differences between identical twins are mostly the result of environmental influences rather than genetic inheritance.

ACTIVITIES

42. Associate each of these statements with the first meiotic division or the second meiotic division, as appropriate:

  a. The pairs of homologous chromosomes line up across the equator of the cell.
  b. Sister chromatids of each chromosome separate.
  c. The two members of each pair of homologous chromosomes separate.
  d. Four haploid cells are created with half the number of chromosomes as the mother cell.
  e. Crossing over brings together segments of chromatids of homologous chromosomes.

43. How many chromatids do meiotic chromosomes have in prophase I? How many do they have in telophase I? Why?

44. Describe the process represented by the following image. Then, answer the question below.

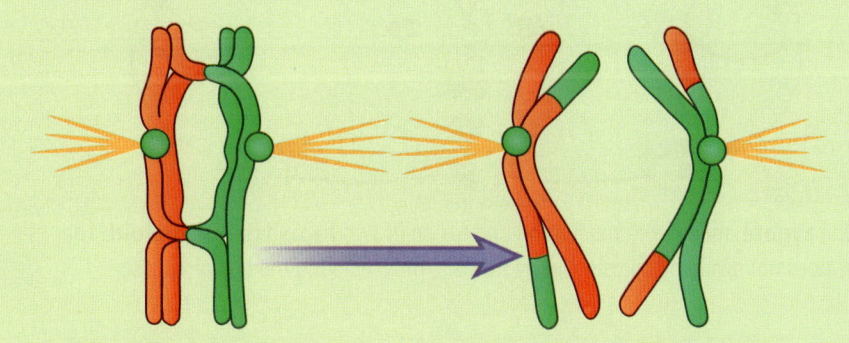

What is the consequence of this phenomenon for the information contained in the DNA?

45. Taking into account the independent assortment of homologous chromosomes in meiosis, would it be correct to say that a father will give his child a copy of half of the chromosomes that he received from his father and half that he received from his mother? Explain your answer.

UNIT 02 **Cell reproduction**

6. Life cycles

> What type of life cycle do humans have?

A **life cycle** is the series of changes that an organism undergoes throughout its life, from birth until reproduction. The cycles of different organisms differ in the types of reproduction and the duration of the haploid and diploid phases. This helps determine three types of life cycles in sexual reproduction: diploid, haploid and haploid-diploid.

PREDOMINANTLY DIPLOID CYCLE

This cycle is typical of **animals**. The diploid phase predominates over the haploid phase, and reproduction is always sexual. The general process of gamete formation is called **gametogenesis**: **oogenesis** in females and **spermatogenesis** in males.

The **haploid** phase only occurs in **gametes** and the cells that produce them.

The rest of the organisms' cells are **diploid** and are called **somatic cells**.

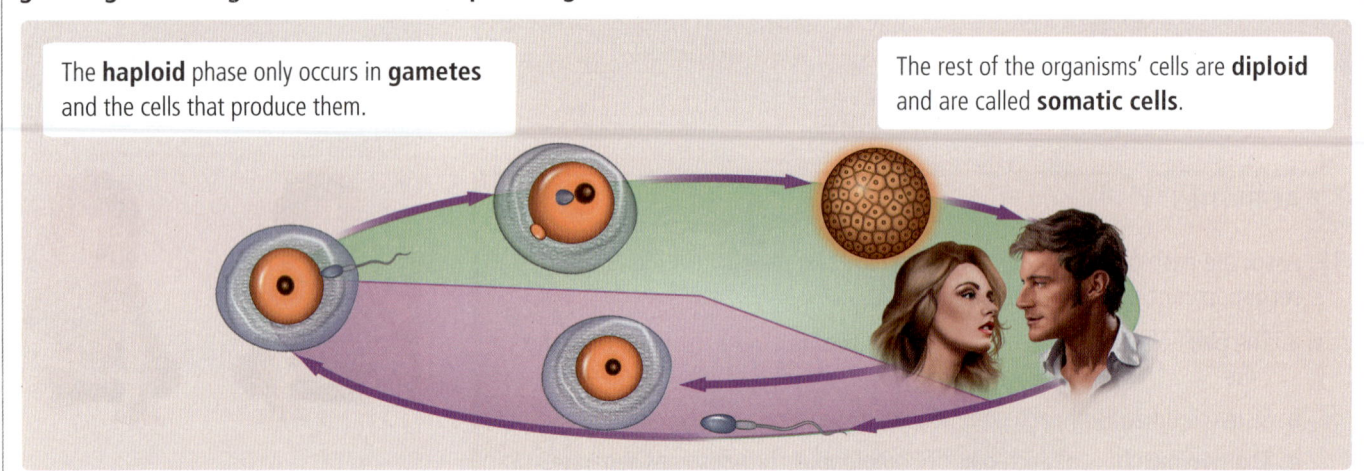

PREDOMINANTLY HAPLOID CYCLE

This occurs in the majority of **fungi** and **algae**. The haploid phase predominates and reproduction can be sexual or asexual.

In green algae from the genus *Chlamydomonas*, organisms are unicellular and haploid, and reproduce by mitosis. The organisms are indistinguishable from the gametes as both have two flagella and look the same. There are complementary mating types, represented by the signs + and –. Descendants from the same line of cells do not mate with each other.

These organisms are in the **haploid** phase for most of their lives.

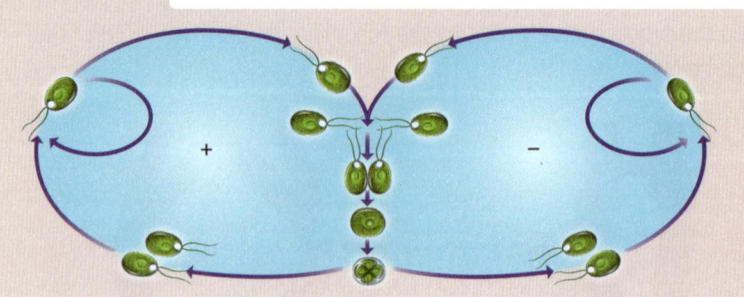

Only the **zygote**, made from the mating and fusion of two haploid cells, is **diploid**. The zygote does not divide by mitosis, but by meiosis, thus restoring the haploid phase.

ACTIVITIES

46. Develop a hypothesis as to why the descendants from the same line of cells of *Chlamydomonas* do not mate with each other.

HAPLOID-DIPLOID CYCLE

This type of cycle appears in certain **plants**, **algae** and **fungi**. It has two generations, one haploid and one diploid. The greater or lesser predominance of each generation varies depending on the group studied.

HAPLOID-DIPLOID CYCLE IN FERNS

In ferns, the two generations are multicellular. The diploid generation (2n) is known as a **sporophyte**, and includes roots, rhizomes and fronds.

On the underside of the fronds are structures called **sporangia**, inside which spores are formed by meiosis.

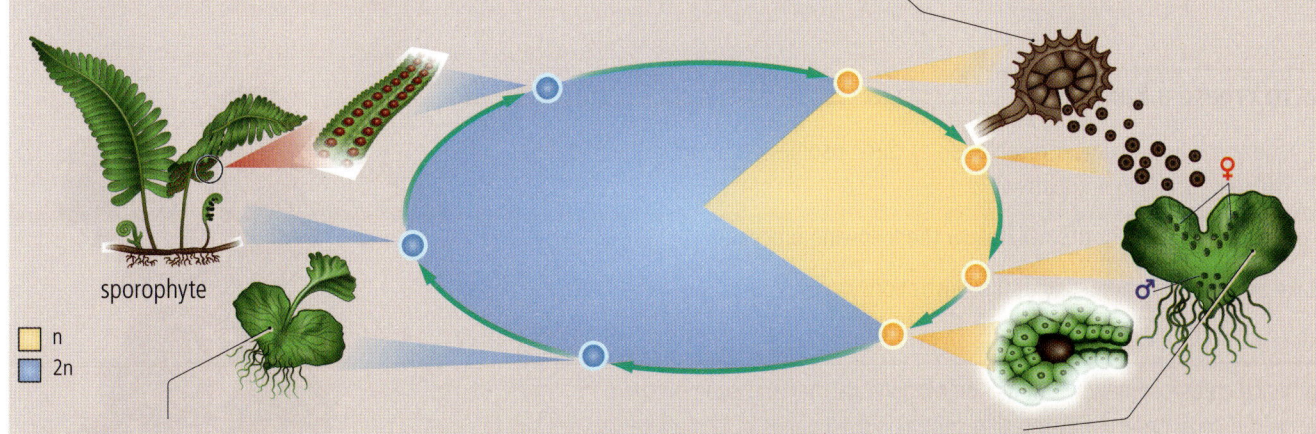

- n
- 2n

sporophyte

The fusion of antherozoid and ova produces a **diploid zygote** which, by mitosis, generates the sporophyte again.

Wind transports the **spores**, which, given they land in a suitable place, divide by successive mitoses to produce a small mass of cells known as a **prothallus** (n) or **haploid gametophyte**. This generation is usually microscopic.

Each gametophyte contains two different structures called **antheridia** (♂) and **archegonia** (♀). The antherozoids are formed in the antheridia and the ova are formed in the archegonia, both without the need for meiosis.

HAPLOID-DIPLOID CYCLE IN ANGIOSPERMS

In angiosperm plants, the haploid generation (gametophyte) is smaller and hidden in the sporophyte, to which it remains attached.

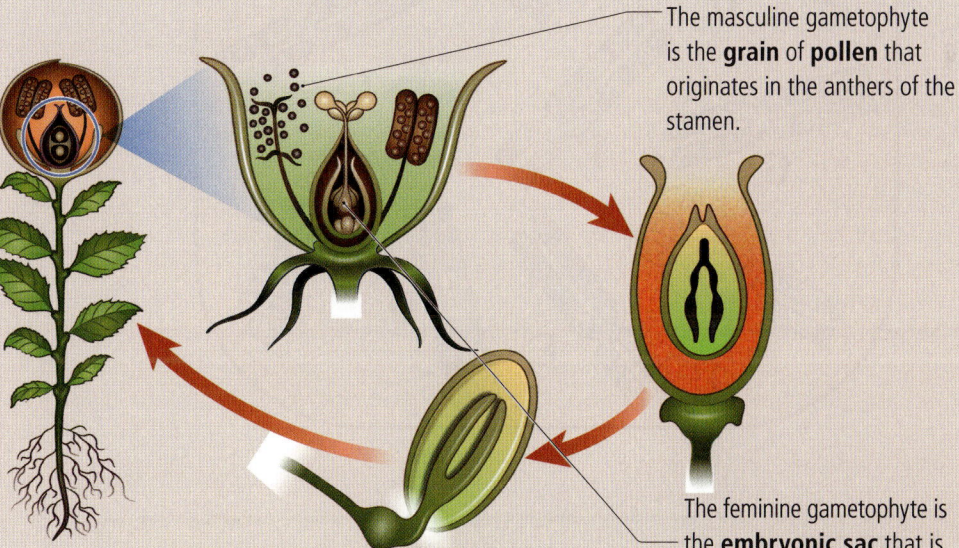

The masculine gametophyte is the **grain** of **pollen** that originates in the anthers of the stamen.

sporophyte

The feminine gametophyte is the **embryonic sac** that is formed inside the pistil.

ACTIVITIES

47. Decide whether a holm oak leaf is a sporophyte or a gametophyte. Justify your answer.

48. State whether the spores of ferns and the cells of the prothallus are haploid or diploid, and explain the reason.

Discovery techniques

MAKING A KARYOTYPE

> How is a karyotype made?

A karyotype is an organized profile of an organism's chromosomes. Metaphase cells are required to prepare a standard karyotype, and virtually any population of dividing cells could be used.

How to create a karyotype

The image below is a visual representation of chromosomes obtained in the metaphase of a cell, with a typical banding pattern.

To create the karyotype of this cell, follow the following process:

1. Make an enlarged photocopy of the illustration.

2. Cut out the chromosomes.

3. Pair each chromosome up with its homologous partner and position them in descending size order, similar to that shown in the images of human karyotypes on page 40.

4. If you can identify the sex chromosomes, place them to one side.

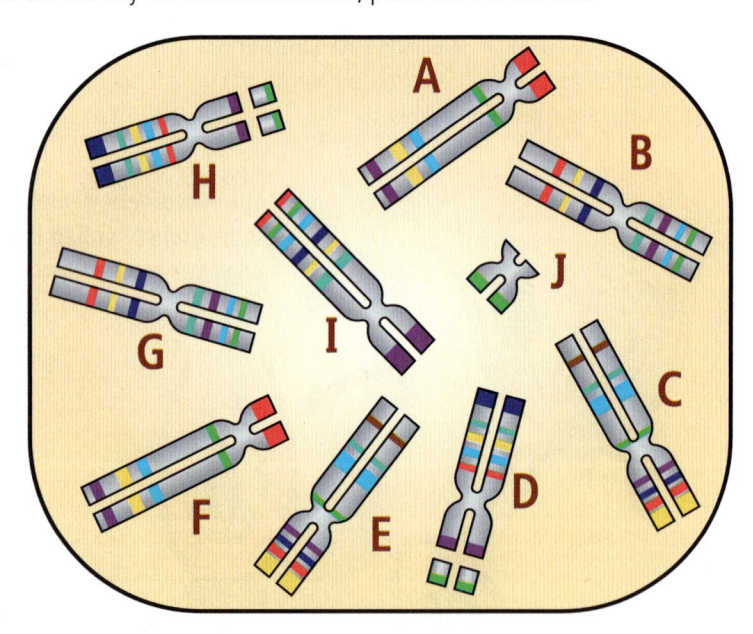

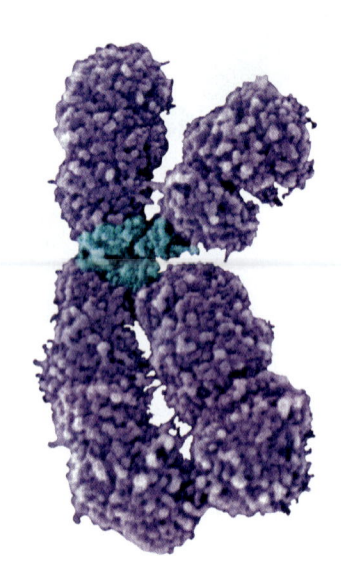

ACTIVITIES

1. Is it a haploid or a diploid cell? Why?

2. Indicate its diploid (2n) and haploid (n) numbers.

3. Does it relate to the heterogametic or the homogametic sex? How did you reach this conclusion?

4. If you have to perform a karyotype of a species, which cells would you use, those in interphase or those in M phase? Explain your answer.

Discovery techniques

OBSERVING MITOSIS IN PLANT CELLS

> How can we observe cells in mitosis?

The tips of growing onion roots are used to observe cells in mitosis because this area contains constantly dividing cells. Specific **dyes** can be used to stain the genetic material for observation.

Prior to this, an onion must be placed in a beaker of water in a well-lit place. It must be left to rest for a few days until the roots are 1–2 cm long.

AIMS

> Make preparations of growing onion tissue and observe the cells in mitosis under a microscope.

MATERIALS

- an onion
- microscope
- slides and coverslips
- wooden tongs
- lancet and blade
- beaker
- spirit burner
- pipette and filter paper
- cedar oil
- nail polish and glycerine
- acetic-orcein and hydrochloric acid (mix 10 mL of acetic-orcein with 0.5 mL of hydrochloric acid 1N)

PROCEDURE

1. On a slide, and with the lancet, cut several slices from the onion as thinly as possible. Prepare several slides with four or five slices taken at varying distances from the tip of the root.

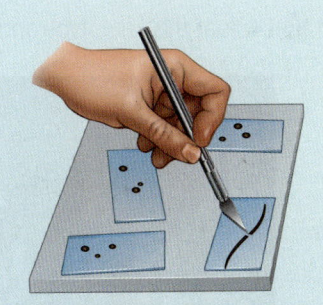

2. Add some drops of acetic-orcein and leave them to act for 15 minutes. Take the slide with the tongs and repeatedly wave it over the spirit burner for two to three minutes. Do not let it boil or you will have to start from the beginning again.

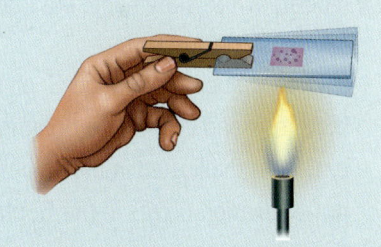

3. Leave it to cool and press a coverslip over the top. Wrap it in filter paper so that the dye does not come into contact with your skin, as it is toxic. Place the preparation under the microscope and focus the lens with the lowest magnifying power.

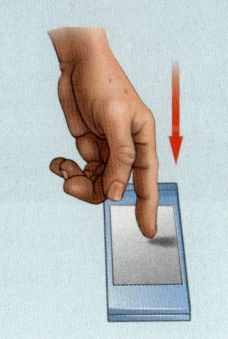

4. Add a drop of cedar oil onto the coverslip and use the immersion lens. To make the preparations last longer, leave them to dry and add a drop of glycerine. Place a coverslip on top and seal the edges with **nail varnish**.

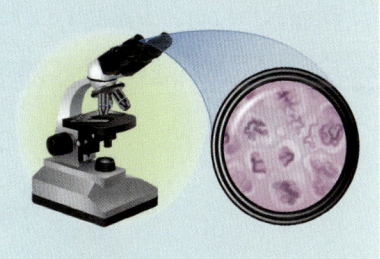

CONCLUSIONS

1. Identify the different phases of mitosis in your preparations and draw the preparations which best show each phase.

2. In which phase is it easier to count the chromosomes? Determine the number of chromosomes in the species observed.

3. Compare the preparations you have made from slices at varying distances from the tip of the root. At what distance is it most common to find dividing cells?

4. Can you see nucleoli in any of the preparations?

Revision activities

1. Discuss with your classmates the advantages and disadvantages of asexual reproduction, comparing it with sexual reproduction.

2. Four successive processes occur in sexual reproduction: gametogenesis, fertilisation, embryonic development and post-embryonic development. Do these processes occur in a hermaphroditic species? Explain your answer.

3. The diagram represents a type of cell reproduction. Is it sexual or asexual? What is it called? Name various organisms that reproduce in this way.

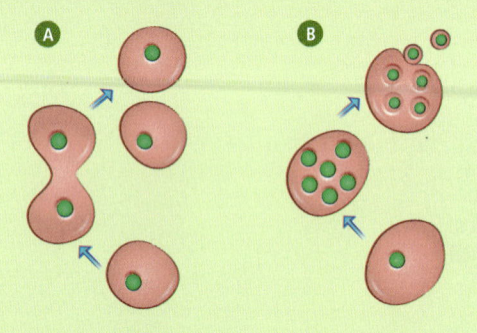

4. Why is it often said that asexual species are particularly sensitive to hostile environmental changes?

5. Indicate which statements are true and which are false. Justify your answers.
   a. DNA is duplicated in the G_1 phase.
   b. Mitosis and cytokinesis occur in the interphase.
   c. DNA is duplicated in the S phase.
   d. Cell division occurs in the G_2 phase.

6. State at which point DNA is duplicated in the cell cycle. What is the purpose of this duplication?

7. Copy and label the following diagram. Then, answer the questions.

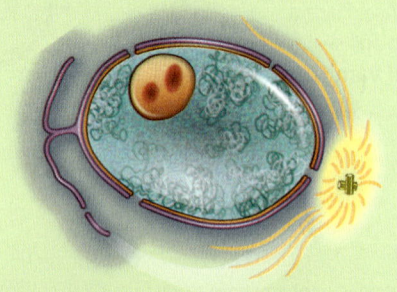

   a. Does it show a nucleus in interphase or a dividing nucleus?
   b. On what are you basing your answer?

8. Search through different resources for information on the type of RNA synthesised in the nucleoli.

9. Is a chromosome the same as a chromatid? Why?

10. What is the relationship between the following terms: DNA, chromatin and chromosome?

11. What happens to chromosomes during mitotic interphase?

12. What is meant by a cell being diploid? And likewise if it is haploid? Give an example of both types of cells.

13. Do you think that there is a link between the number of chromosomes of a species and its degree of evolution? Justify your answer.

14. Are homologous chromosomes totally identical molecules of DNA? Explain your answer.

15. How would you differentiate a metacentric chromosome from a telocentric one? And likewise, how would you differentiate a submetacentric chromosome from an acrocentric one?

16. Look at this karyotype and answer the following questions.

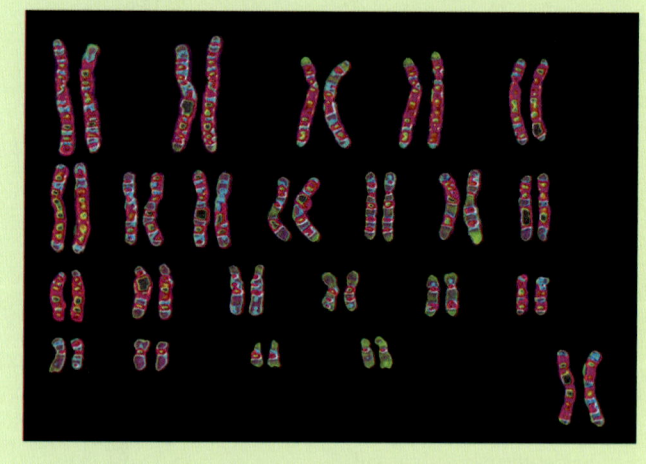

    a. How many chromosomes does this species have? And what is the number of pairs of homologous chromosomes?
    b. Has it been obtained from a sex cell or a somatic cell? Why?
    c. Decide whether the karyotype belongs to a homogametic or a heterogametic organism and explain why.

17. Develop a hypothesis that explains the fact that many organisms have diploid and haploid cells.

18 Decide whether the following statement is true or false and explain why.

Each human cell contains 46 chromosomes in total, 23 of maternal origin and 23 of paternal origin.

19 Appropriately assign each of the following statements to prophase, metaphase, anaphase or telophase in mitosis:

a. A new cell membrane forms around each set of daughter chromosomes.

b. The completely condensed chromosomes line up across the equator of the cell.

c. The daughter chromosomes are slowly transported to opposing ends of the mother cell.

d. The nuclear membrane ruptures.

20 List the differences between cell division in prokaryotic and eukaryotic organisms.

21 Cytokinesis is different in plant cells than in animal cells. What is the reason for this? Explain the differences.

22 Briefly explain how the packaging of DNA gives rise to chromosomes.

23 How many chromatids do chromosomes have in the prophase of mitosis? How many do they have in telophase? Why?

24 Make a comparative summary of the differences between meiosis and mitosis.

25 What would happen if meiosis did not exist in organisms that reproduce sexually?

26 Explain the following statement:
Mitosis is conservative, whereas meiosis is reductive.

27 In fruit flies or vinegar flies (*Drosophila melanogaster*), the heterogametic sex is the male. Below are the chromosomes of a male and a female. Which corresponds to each sex? Justify your answer.

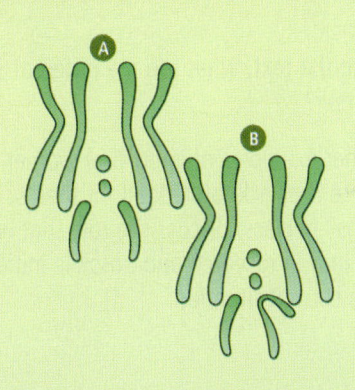

28 Which of the following statements are true? Correct any which are false.

a. In the prophase of plant cells, the centrosomes, duplicated in interphase, are located at opposite poles of the spindle.

b. In metaphase, microtubules joined to the centromere pull the sister chromatids towards the poles.

c. In anaphase II, homologous chromosomes separate and become daughter chromosomes.

d. New nuclei are formed at the end of telophase.

29 State how many chromatids a chromosome has in the following phases:

a. Anaphase of mitosis
b. Prophase of mitosis
c. Anaphase I of meiosis
d. Prophase I of meiosis
e. Anaphase II of meiosis
f. Prophase II of meiosis

30 Sort each of the following statements into prophase I, metaphase I, anaphase I, telophase I or the second division of meiosis:

a. The two sister chromatids of each chromosome are separated.

b. The microtubules of the spindle drag the two members of each pair of homologous chromosomes to opposite poles.

c. The pairs of homologous chromosomes line up across the equator.

d. Each nucleus has a haploid number of chromosomes with two chromatids.

e. The chromosomes, with two chromatids each, attach strongly to their homologous partners while condensing at the same time.

31 Identify and correct any incorrect statements:

a. Mitosis is related to the development of multicellular organisms.

b. A human diploid cell has 46 chromosomes.

c. Meiosis is related to cell reproduction.

d. Mitosis is the type of cell division that occurs in the growth of tumours.

e. Human ova are haploid cells that contain 23 chromosomes.

32 If a diploid organism has 30 chromosomes, how many chromosomes would its gametes have? How many would the zygotes created from fertilisation of these gametes have? Explain your answer.

33 Explain with a drawing what crossing over is.

Read and think

MARGARITA SALAS: THE SUCCESS OF A PIONEER

Margarita Salas was born in Asturias in 1938. She was one of the first women who graduated from university in chemistry, which she studied at the Universidad Complutense de Madrid. She then decided to **pursue** a **PhD** under the direction of Alberto Sols, a biochemistry pioneer in Spain. She **was** truly **ahead of her time**, in a period when doing research in Spain was a very difficult task, and something unheard of for a woman.

In 1963, after finishing her doctoral thesis, Salas moved to New York with her husband, Eladio Viñuela, who was also a scientist. Both of them stayed in the United States for four years, working at Severo Ochoa's laboratory at New York University.

When she came back to Spain, Salas started her own research group at the Universidad Complutense de Madrid and taught molecular genetics there from 1968 to 1992. She designed the contents of the course herself, with the help of her husband, bringing to Spain all the new knowledge they had acquired during their time in the US.

She then moved on to work at the Molecular Biology Centre, a mixed institute of the Universidad Autónoma de Madrid and the Spanish National Research Council. To date, she still works in the laboratory every day, training new generations of young scientists. She remains the only Spanish female scientist to be a member of the US National Academy of Sciences and the Royal Spanish Academy, amongst many other institutions. Despite all her achievements, Salas admits she has felt discriminated against for being a woman throughout her career.

Her most renowned scientific contribution was the discovery and characterization of the DNA polymerase of the phi 29 bacteriophages. Phi 29 is a virus that infects some kinds of bacteria. This virus only has 20 genes and, by studying them, Salas, her team, and many other researchers discovered how DNA works, how genes code for proteins and how those proteins are related to each other to form a functional virus.

However, Salas' most important discovery was the identification of phi 29's DNA polymerase. DNA polymerases are enzymes that are essential for the duplication of DNA during the cell cycle. Phi 29's DNA polymerase was exceptionally fast in duplicating even tiny amounts of DNA. This is why it became a key enzyme for biotechnology research all over the world.

The fact that Salas characterized and patented this DNA polymerase was extremely important. An American company bought the license and developed DNA amplification kits that are used in laboratories worldwide. Moreover, the Spanish National Research Council has received over 4 million euros (more than 50% of its royalty income) from this patent, making it the most profitable patent in the history of Spain.

Beyond a shadow of a doubt, Margarita Salas is one of the most important figures in Spanish science. By tirelessly devoting herself to the study of basic science, she has contributed to the development of biotechnology all around the world. She has also achieved what is the most important example of transfer of knowledge from the laboratory bench to industry to date in Spain.

ANSWER THE QUESTIONS

1. From what you know, in which stage of the cell cycle do you think DNA polymerase plays a role? Explain what happens in that stage using your own words.
2. Explain the main differences between mitosis and meiosis. Do you think DNA polymerase is required for both to take place?
3. What makes phi 29 so valuable for research?
4. According to the text, what are the different stages of a research career?
5. Look for other examples of important women in science. Were they acknowledged for their scientific contributions? In class, discuss the role that women play and should play in research and possible initiatives to improve the current situation.

Work it out

CONCEPT MAP

Use the words in the word cloud to create your own unit map in your notebook. Write any connecting texts you need.

metaphase
mitosis
cell division
DNA packaging (chromosomes)
first meiotic division
genetically identical daughter cells
nuclear division
Cell cycle
genetically different daughter cells (n)
second meiotic division
protein synthesis
telophase
DNA duplication
interphase
prophase
meiosis
anaphase
DNA in chromatin form
cytokinesis
cytoplasmic division

SELF-ASSESSMENT

Carry out a self-assessment of what you learned in this unit. Choose one answer for each question and then check your answers.

1 Which of the following is not a type of asexual reproduction?
   a. Budding
   b. Dissemination
   c. Binary fission

2 What is the correct order of the phases of the eukaryotic cell cycle?
   a. M phase, G_1 phase, S phase, G_2 phase
   b. S phase, G_1 phase, M phase, G_2 phase
   c. M phase, G_1 phase, G_2 phase, S phase

3 What is a G_0 phase?
   a. A very fast S phase
   b. A very short G_2 phase
   c. A very long G_1 phase

4 Which of the following can only be seen in a dividing nucleus?
   a. Nucleoli
   b. Packaged chromosomes
   c. Nucleoplasm

5 What is a chromatid?
   a. The end part of a chromosome
   b. The constricted region separating chromosome arms
   c. Each half of a chromosome

6 What is the correct order of the different phases of mitosis?
   a. Prophase, anaphase, metaphase, telophase
   b. Prophase, metaphase, anaphase, telophase
   c. Anaphase, metaphase, prophase, telophase

7 Which cell type requires the Golgi body for cytokinesis?
   a. Plant cells
   b. Animal cells
   c. Prokaryotic cells

8 Which of the following is false?
   a. Human gametes are haploid.
   b. DNA duplicates twice during meiosis.
   c. Mitosis produces two daughter cells.

9 How many different gametes can a given human generate?
   a. 2^{46}
   b. 2^4
   c. 2^{23}

10 Which of these statements is false?
   a. Humans have a diploid life cycle.
   b. All fungi have a haploid life cycle.
   c. Ferns have a haploid-diploid life cycle.

Earth dynamics

03 The inheritance of traits

<<LOOKING BACK

- What is the function of genetic material?
- Why is meiosis important in sexual reproduction?
- In the human species, males are known as the 'heterogametic sex' and females as the 'homogametic sex'. What does this mean?
- What is the difference between autosomes and heterochromosomes?
- What is a sex-linked disorder? Can you give an example?

P

X

F_1

'Top model' organisms

Fruit flies (*Drosophila melanogaster*) are annoying to most people – they don't just love your favourite snacks, but also crawl all over the screen when you're watching TV at night! However, ask any geneticist in the world and they'll tell you that *Drosophila melanogaster* is the greatest insect ever.

For more than 100 years, fruit flies have been considered a 'model organism' – that is, a species which is studied to understand the biology of other organisms, including humans. They share 75% of the genes that cause human diseases, and fruit fly research is shining a light on Alzheimer's and Parkinson's, cancer and diabetes, and even issues like drug abuse and aging!

There are lots of advantages to studying fruit flies. They are extremely cheap and easy to store and feed, and because their genome is so well understood, researchers can even cause them to develop unusual characteristics, like oddly shaped wings or different coloured eyes – even no eyes at all!

- Experimenting on other creatures is very controversial – but not in this case! Why?
- Why do you think scientists might want to manipulate fruit flies' appearance?
- A female fruit fly can lay 100 eggs a day, up to 2 000 in her lifetime, and the period between generations is only ten days. How does this benefit research?
- What disadvantages do you think other kinds of lab organisms might have?

Four o'clock flower
(*Mirabilis jalapa*)

LOOKING FORWARD >>

- How did the study of genetics begin?
- What is the difference between genotype and phenotype?
- What do Mendel's laws state?
- What is incomplete dominance?
- Where are genes found?
- What types of gametes does an organism with genotype Aa produce?
- Is the Rh factor dominant or recessive?
- What is the test cross used for?

1. The birth of genetics

> How did the study of genetics begin?

Ever since the Neolithic Period, with the appearance of agriculture and cattle farming, humans have been selecting reproductive individuals and seeds to perpetuate a series of desirable features in offspring. This is how they have achieved breeds that produce more milk or varieties that give more appetising fruit.

Despite the knowledge gained through these age-old activities, the mechanism of the inheritance of traits of living organisms was not understood until the end of the 19th century, when genetics became a scientific discipline.

> **HYBRIDISATION**
>
> In hermaphrodite flowering plants, **hybridisation** consists of cutting stamens before they mature, and pollinating the flowers with pollen from another plant of the same or different species.

MENDEL'S WORK

Through simple plant hybridisation experiments, the Austrian monk **Gregor Johann Mendel** (1822–1884) rejected the then-accepted doctrine of **blending inheritance**. This stated that offspring, having received an equal share of inheritance from the father and the mother, must present an intermediate trait of the two presented by its parents.

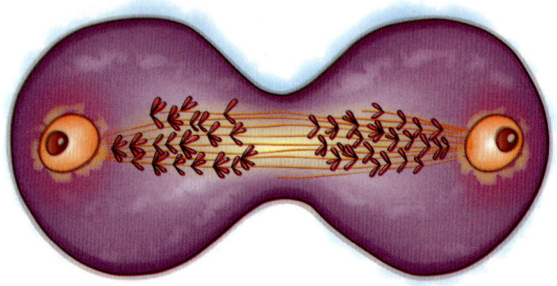

◀ Mendel proposed the existence of hereditary particulates, which he called **hereditary factors** (now known as genes). These factors are responsible for the manifestation of a certain characteristic and can be observed through generations.

▶ The study of **a unique trait** was his best decision as, until then, scientists who experimented with plants observed offspring as a whole, instead of concentrating on isolated traits.

The results of his experiments were published in 1866 in the Proceedings of the Natural History Society of Brno with the title *Experiments on Plant Hybridisation*. However, his work was not recognised until its rediscovery in 1900 by **Hugo de Vries** (1848–1935), **Carl Correns** (1864–1933) and **Erick von Tschermak** (1871–1962), who, independently, came to the same conclusions while working on other species of plants. Mendel's initial publication has been considered the cornerstone of genetics ever since.

With Mendel's experiments, the phenomenon of biological inheritance began to be explained scientifically, and the laws which govern the mechanism of the transmission of biological traits from generation to generation started to be understood. Therefore, it can be said that genetics was born from his work, although this term was not used until 1906 when the British biologist **William Bateson** (1861–1926) defined it for the first time as 'the science that studies the inheritance and variation of living organisms'.

ACTIVITIES

1. In scientific literature the year 1900 is talked about as 'the year in which Mendel's laws were rediscovered'. What is meant by this?

2. Search for information in different resources and check whether Mendel's experiments were the first to use the hybridisation technique.

2 Fundamental concepts of genetics

> **What is the difference between genotype and phenotype?**

To understand Mendel's work, you need to know a series of basic concepts.

- **Allelomorphic genes**. For any characteristic, there is a pair of hereditary factors known as 'allelomorphic genes', or simply **alleles**, which come from each of the parents. On forming the gametes, the two alleles separate, with each gamete receiving one allele from each pair.

- **Dominance and recessiveness**. Although each pair of alleles determines a certain trait, each of them can have a different relationship of dominance over the other.

The **dominant allele** always manifests itself in an individual. It is represented by capital letters (for example, **A**).

AA

The **recessive allele** only manifests itself in the absence of the dominant allele. It is represented by lower caps (for example, **a**).

aa

- **Purebreds and hybrids**. As each individual has a maternal allele and a paternal allele, they will produce two types of individuals: homozygotes or heterozygotes.

Homozygotes or **purebreds** are individuals that have **two of the same alleles** for the same trait. They are represented by two of the same letters, in capitals or lower caps (for example, **AA**, **aa**, **BB**, **bb**).

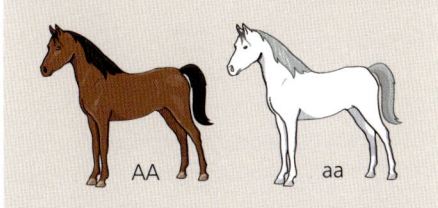

AA   aa

Heterozygotes or **hybrids** are individuals that have **two different alleles** for the same trait. They are represented by two of the same letters, one in capitals and the other in lower caps (for example, **Aa**, **Bb**).

Aa

- **Genotype and phenotype**. The dominance relationships between alleles and the influence of **environmental factors** make individuals with the same genes manifest different traits. Although genes are primarily responsible for traits, environmental factors also affect their expression.

The **genotype** is the set of **genes** that an individual receives from its parents.

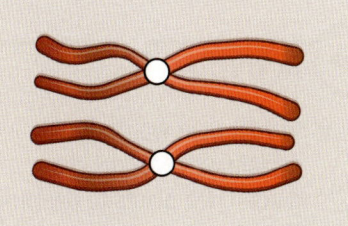

The **phenotype** is the set of **visible traits** of an organism.

ACTIVITIES

3. Until the 19th century, the blending theory of inheritance was accepted. Search different resources for information on this and explain why this theory was abandoned after Gregor Mendel's discoveries.

4. What is the difference between a dominant and a recessive allele?

5. Search for various examples that help to understand the concepts of genotype and phenotype.

2.1 Model organisms

These are non-human species that are used in the laboratory to help scientists understand biological processes. Examples of model organisms to study genetics are garden pea plants and common fruit flies.

MENDEL'S PEA PLANTS

Mendel selected the garden pea plant (*Pisum sativum*) for his experiments, but why did he choose peas? There are several advantages of using garden peas in genetics:

- This plant is **easy to cultivate** and produces a large number of offspring.
- Pea flowers naturally **self-pollinate**, meaning that the pollen produced by a hermaphrodite flower pollinates the pistil of the same flower. Therefore, **cross-pollinating** between different plants only occurs when performed by the researcher.
- **Pure-breeding varieties** are already established and they present the same trait generation after generation: one type always produces yellow seeds, another produces green seeds, etc.
- Traits with two variants are easily **distinguishable upon observation**. Seed colour is green or yellow, and flowers are white or purple. Therefore, intermediate traits do not exist.

○ *Pisum sativum*

COLOUR TRAIT OF *Pisum sativum* SEEDS

The garden pea's seed colour is controlled by a gene that has two allelic variants: one responsible for the colour yellow and another for green.

The allele determining the colour yellow, **A**, is dominant over the allele determining green, **a**. Therefore, heterozygotic individuals **Aa** only express the colour yellow, while the homozygotes can be either **AA**, which are yellow, or **aa**, which are green.

The dominance relationship between different alleles of the same gene means that two different genotypes for seed colour, **AA** and **Aa**, produce the same phenotype of the colour yellow.

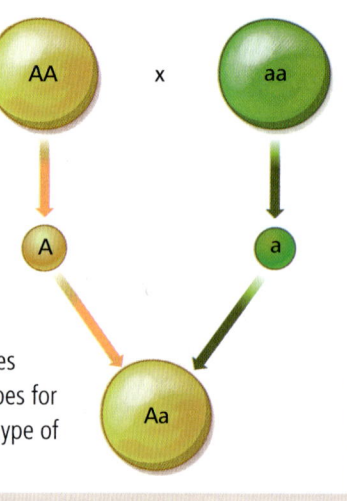

THE 'STAR' OF GENETICS

Although Aristotle had already mentioned the small fly that, by his account, was created from vinegar, the 'common fruit fly' or 'vinegar fly' (*Drosophila melanogaster*) was described for the first time at the beginning of the 19th century. It soon made its appearance in different universities, because of its special properties, for studying the inheritance of traits:

- It is small and easy to breed in laboratories.
- It reproduces all year round.
- It produces a generation every twelve days.
- It can produce up to 400 eggs each time it lays.
- Males and females are easy to tell apart.
- It has a small number of chromosomes ($n = 4$).

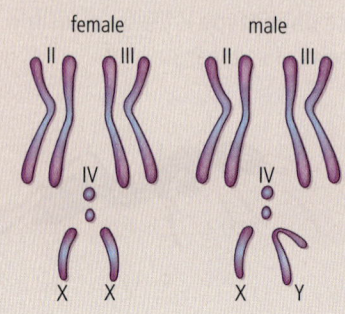

BIG THINKER

Gregor Mendel is known as the 'Father of modern genetics', but he lived a more humble life than that title suggests. Son of a peasant farmer, he worked as a beekeeper as a child. He went to the University of Vienna to study botany, zoology, history, maths and physics – but left to join a monastery and became a monk! While working as a teacher, he grew peas for fifteen years and gradually realised that characteristics of the plants were passed down between each generation. Mendel named all his plants, as if they were pets – but how can you remember 30 000 names?

ACTIVITIES

6. In your own words, briefly explain why Mendel chose garden pea plants to perform his experiments.

3. Mendel's laws

> What do Mendel's laws state?

Gregor Mendel laid the foundations for current genetics by studying the transmission of certain traits with contrasting variants in garden peas (*Pisum sativum*), such as seed colour and texture, flower colour and position, **pod** colour and shape, and stalk length.

The method used by Mendel included the following experiments.

1 Mendel artificially cross-pollinated the **parental generation** (P ♂ × P ♀) of two pure-breeding varieties with one or various contrasting traits. For each trait studied, one parent is dominant and the other is recessive. Mendel called them **contrasting traits**.

2 He observed the phenotype of the offspring, known as the **first filial generation** or F_1, looking at the expression of the traits of the parents and noting down the results.

3 He allowed the F_1 plants to self-pollinate. This produced what is known as the **second filial generation** or F_2. He noted the number of offspring that expressed each examined trait.

4 He repeated the self-pollination with the seeds of the F_2 generation to obtain the **third filial generation** or F_3.

5 The results of his experiments, interpreted logically and from a mathematical perspective, led Mendel to demonstrate the existence of hereditary factors (genes), and to understand their behaviour over generations.

Thanks to his experiments, Mendel could establish three basic principles on the inheritance of traits. One of the scientists who rediscovered his work, Carl Correns, called these principles **Mendel's laws**.

ACTIVITIES

7. Indicate which of the following statements are false, and correct them.
   a. Mendel stated that having received an equal hereditary contribution from the father and the mother, the offspring presented intermediate traits to those expressed by their parents.
   b. A few days after the publication of the results of his experiments in 1886, Mendel received worldwide scientific recognition, given that his discoveries were a turning point for the future of biology.
   c. Mendel's best decision was to observe the traits of plants overall and not in an isolated fashion, as had been done up until that point.

8. Did Mendel use the term *gene* to refer to hereditary particulates? Explain your answer.

9. Write a small summary of the method used by Mendel in his experiments.

10. Describe what the letter P and the expressions F_1, F_2 and F_3 mean in classical genetics.

3.1 Mendel's first law

Mendel cross-pollinated pure-breeding plants with green seeds with pure-breeding plants with yellow seeds. The F_1 generation was **homogeneous**, or rather, all the seeds were yellow. He concluded that the determining factor of the yellow colour trait was dominant over the factor that determines the green colour trait.

He repeated the experiment with a further six contrasting traits, and in all the cases, he confirmed the **F_1 generation to be uniform**, or homogeneous in terms of the examined traits. All of the plants manifested the traits of one of the parents, the **dominant trait**.

> **SEX OF PARENTS**
> Mendel confirmed in his experiments that the same results were obtained **regardless of** the sex of the parents. In other words, it made no difference whether the grain of pollen or the ovule provided the dominant trait.

	seed colour	seed shape	flower colour	flower position	pod colour	pod shape	stalk length
dominant	yellow	round	purple	axial	green	inflated	tall
recessive	green	wrinkled	white	terminal	yellow	constricted	short
P							
X							
P							
F_1	all yellow seeds	all round seeds	all purple flowers	all axial flowers	all green pods	all inflated pods	all long stalks

Mendel's first law, or the **uniformity of hybrids**, states that, when two purebreds are crossed for a contrasting trait, all of the descendants express the dominant trait.

ACTIVITIES

11. Explain why the F_1 generation produced from crossing two pure-breeding varieties is uniform.

12. Give various different examples (other than the colour of pea seeds) to explain the concepts of recessive alleles and dominant alleles.

13. Did Mendel observe anything about the sex of the parents in the results of his experiments? Explain your answer.

14. Observe the traits of the garden pea that Mendel studied and describe how the first generation would be after crossing the following:

    a. Plants with round seeds and plants with wrinkled seeds.

    b. Plants with tall stalks and plants with short stalks.

3.2 Mendel's second law

Mendel continued with his experiments by planting the seeds obtained and leaving the plants from the F_1 generation to self-pollinate. He confirmed that the F_2 generation was never uniform. There were a large number of seeds with the dominant trait, but also a lesser proportion with the recessive trait, which was hidden in the F1 generation. This led him to believe that the determining factors for each trait were separated when the gametes were formed. He counted the seeds in which each of the traits had appeared and observed that the proportion was 3:1 meaning that for every four seeds in the F_2, generation, three presented the dominant trait and one expressed the recessive trait.

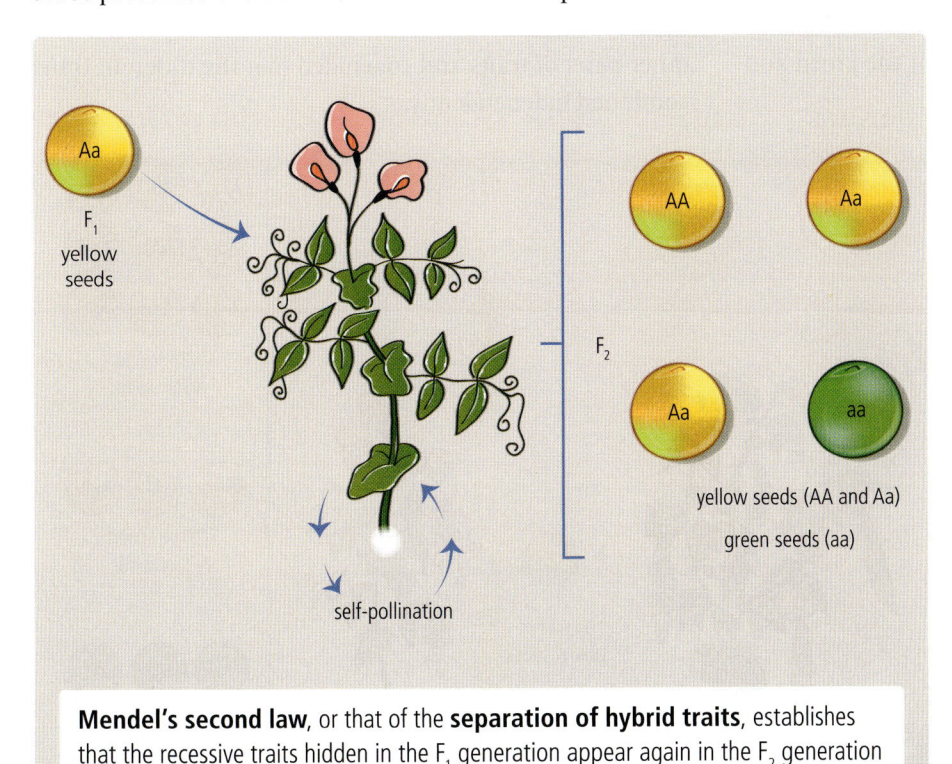

Mendel's second law, or that of the **separation of hybrid traits**, establishes that the recessive traits hidden in the F_1 generation appear again in the F_2 generation in the proportion of three dominants for every recessive (3:1).

◗ LAPLACE'S RULE AND PROBABILITY

The probability of an event happening is calculated by **Laplace's rule**, dividing the number of favourable outcomes by the number of possible outcomes.

Probability of an event = favourable outcomes/possible outcomes

In the case of plants with the genotype Aa, there are two possible cases when the gametes are formed, and one favourable outcome for each allele, so the probability of their being **A** or **a** is 1/2.

The probability of two independent events occurring at the same time is equal to the product of the two individual probabilities. Therefore, in the two independent events of pollen and ovule formation, the probability that a grain of pollen **A** or **a** fertilises an ovule of either type would be 1/2 x 1/2 = 1/4.

	pollen A 1/2	pollen a 1/2
ovule A 1/2	seed AA 1/4	seed Aa 1/4
ovule B 1/2	seed Aa 1/4	seed aa 1/4

With these results, Mendel sensed that, in the F_1 hybrids, the determining factors for each trait were separated when the pollen and ovules formed, so half of the gametes were carriers of the dominant allele and the other half carried the recessive. Then, random assortment determined which of the two types of pollen would unite with each type of ovule.

trait	dominant		recessive		total	ratio
seed colour	yellow	6 022	green	2 001	8 023	3.01:1
seed shape	round	5 474	wrinkled	1 850	7 324	2.96:1
flower colour	purple	705	white	224	929	3.1:1
flower position	axial	651	terminal	207	858	3.14:1
pod colour	green	428	yellow	152	580	2.82:1
pod shape	inflated	882	constricted	299	1 181	2.95:1
stalk length	tall	787	short	277	1 064	2.84:1

◐ The table reflects the results of the experiments Mendel carried out with the seven traits examined in *Pisum sativum*.

ACTIVITIES

15. What are the phenotypes and genotypes resulting from the cross of a pure-breeding *Pisum sativum* with axially-positioned flowers with another pure-breeding variety that has its flowers in a terminal arrangement?

3.3 Mendel's third law

Mendel studied the hybridisation of pure-breeding varieties for more than one trait. He cross-pollinated a pure-breeding line that was dominant for two different traits with another pure-breeding variety that was recessive for the same traits. He took the pollen from the pure-breeding plants with round yellow seeds and pollinated the plants grown from pure-breeding green and wrinkled seeds. The F_1 generation was, as expected, according to the first law: all the seeds were yellow and round. However, although they had a round yellow phenotype, they also carried the factors for the green and wrinkled traits.

When he planted these seeds and left them to grow and self-pollinate to obtain the F_2 generation, he found that four different phenotypes appeared in the proportion 9:3:3:1; in other words, for every sixteen seeds, nine were yellow and round, three were yellow and wrinkled, three were green and round and one was green and wrinkled. This shows that the seed's colour trait (yellow, green) is transmitted independently of the trait for seed shape (round, wrinkled); otherwise, no wrinkled yellow or round green seeds would have appeared. Mendel confirmed that this happened with other pairs of traits and concluded that the different traits combined independently.

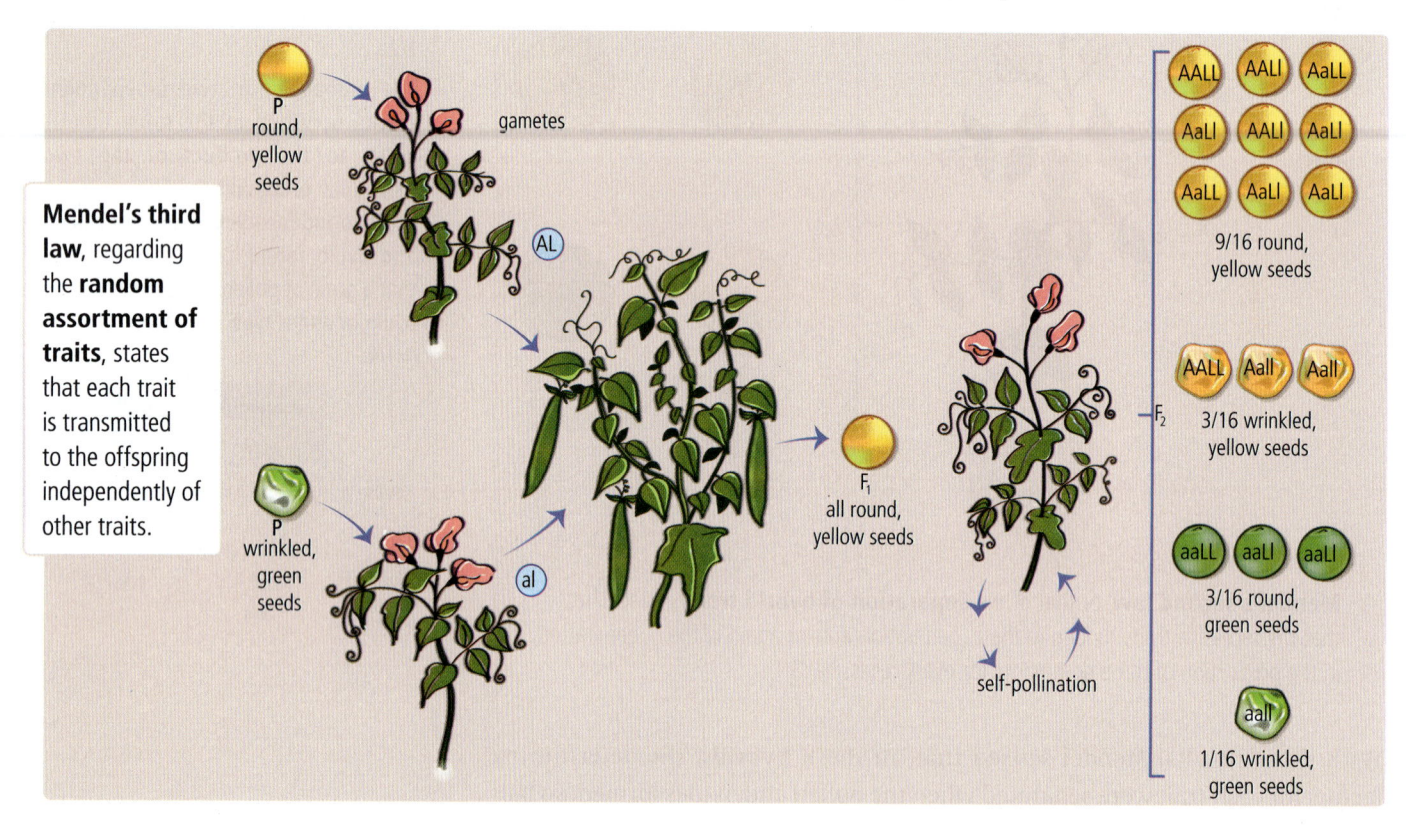

Mendel's third law, regarding the **random assortment of traits**, states that each trait is transmitted to the offspring independently of other traits.

ACTIVITIES

16. Would the yellow-purple garden pea plants of the F_2 generation obtained by Mendel (the product of the self-pollination of the F_1 generation of hybrid yellow seeds) be purebreds? Explain your answer.

17. If Mendel had obtained 344 seeds in the F_2 generation from the self-pollination of the F_1 hybrids, approximately how many seeds would have been green? How many would have been yellow?

18. In an experiment consisting of leaving the plants of the F_1 generation to self-pollinate, 1 296 seeds were obtained in the F_2 generation. According to Mendel's third law, how many would there be of each of the four possible varieties?

19. Explain the outcomes obtained in the F_1 generation by crossing a pure-breeding plant with dominant round yellow seeds with another pure-breeding variety with wrinkled green seeds.

4. Exceptions to Mendel's laws

> What is incomplete dominance?

There are many exceptions to Mendel's laws. However, the detailed study of these exceptions not only reaffirmed the laws, but even improved understanding of the mechanisms of biological inheritance.

This is the case of the discovery of **incomplete dominance**, which occurs when there is a lack of dominance between the alleles of a trait and, therefore, the phenotypes of the two pure-breeding varieties appear to blend. Neither of the two varieties dominates the other, resulting in an intermediate hybrid between the pure-breeding parents. As such, incomplete dominance, unlike dominant inheritance, allows the hybrids to be distinguished from the purebreds by observation alone.

INCOMPLETE DOMINANCE IN PLANTS

The four o'clock flower (*Mirabilis jalapa*) has two pure-breeding varieties in terms of the colour of its flowers. By crossing the pure-breeding red-flowering plants with pure-breeding white-flowering plants, an F_1 generation which only has pink flowers is produced.

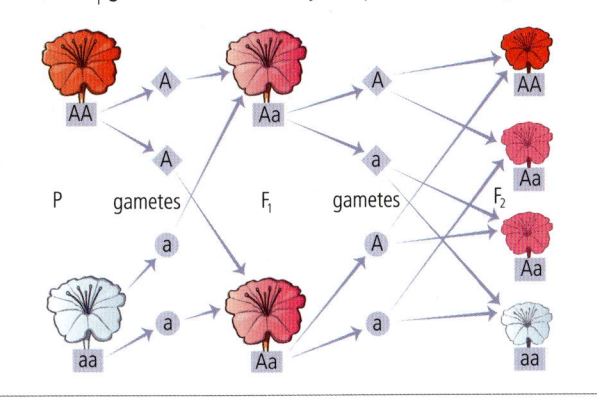

INCOMPLETE DOMINANCE IN ANIMALS

The Andalusian chicken has two pure-breeding varieties in terms of the colour of its feathers. By crossing the pure-breeding black-purple variety with the pure-breeding white-purple variety, homogenous offspring with bluish-grey feathers is produced.

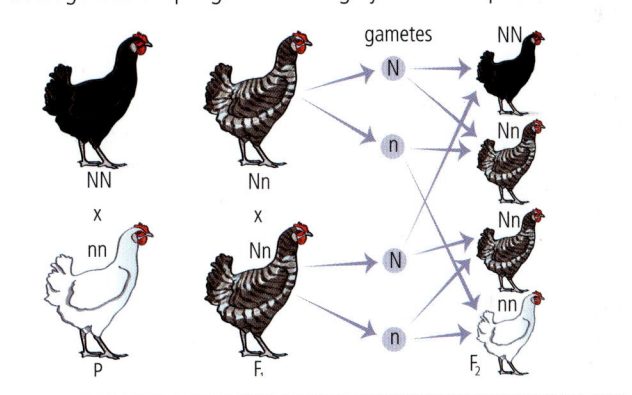

ACTIVITIES

20. In your own words, briefly explain the difference between dominance and incomplete dominance. Give an example to support your explanation.

21. Do you think that the incomplete dominance expressed in the four o'clock flower contradicts Mendel's first law? Support your answer.

22. Indicate the genotype and phenotype proportions that would be obtained by leaving four o'clock flower plants with pink flowers to self-pollinate.

23. By crossing pure-breeding black guinea pigs with albino guinea pigs, all of the offspring are black. If these offspring are allowed to breed amongst themselves, 75% of the offspring are black and the remaining 25% are albino. Represent the combinations and indicate whether they comply with Mendel's laws.

24. Form work groups to investigate any topic related to Mendelian genetics (biography of Mendel, the rediscovery of Mendel's laws, etc.). With the information found, each team will prepare a presentation using a computer programme to give to the rest of their classmates.

5. The chromosomal theory of inheritance

> Where are genes found?

With the discovery of Mendel's laws and the universal acceptance of Mendelism, questions were raised about the location and composition of genes (Mendel's factors) in the cells of living organisms. Information about their location came at almost the same time as the rediscovery of Mendel's laws; but the questions about their composition took decades to be answered.

In the first decade of the 20th century, various scientists observed a parallelism between the behaviour of chromosomes during meiosis and the genes in Mendelian experiments.

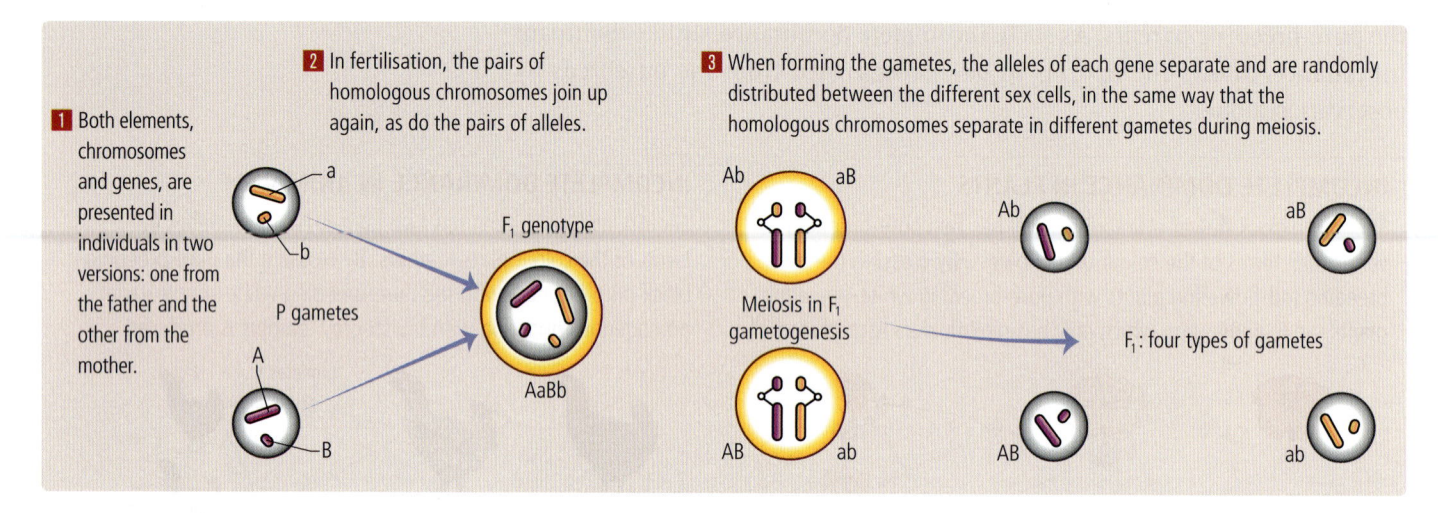

1 Both elements, chromosomes and genes, are presented in individuals in two versions: one from the father and the other from the mother.

2 In fertilisation, the pairs of homologous chromosomes join up again, as do the pairs of alleles.

3 When forming the gametes, the alleles of each gene separate and are randomly distributed between the different sex cells, in the same way that the homologous chromosomes separate in different gametes during meiosis.

In the 1920s, the biologist and geneticist **Thomas Hunt Morgan** (1866–1945) performed a series of experiments on the location of genes.

GENE LINKAGE

Morgan confirmed that many genes are inherited together on the same chromosome. As a result, the proportions were not as expected according to Mendel's third law. He called this phenomenon **gene linkage**, and the genes that were inherited together, **linkage groups**. He demonstrated that the number of linkage groups matched the number of chromosomes.

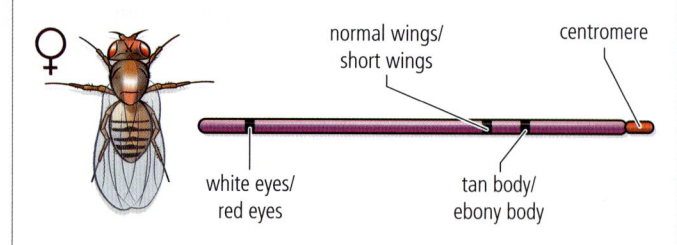

RECOMBINATION AND CROSSING OVER

Morgan also discovered that the genes linked on the same chromosome sometimes behave as if they were not linked, meaning they combine freely as if they were on different chromosomes (**recombination**). He related this phenomenon to the exchange of chromatid segments between homologous chromosomes in meiosis (**crossing over**).

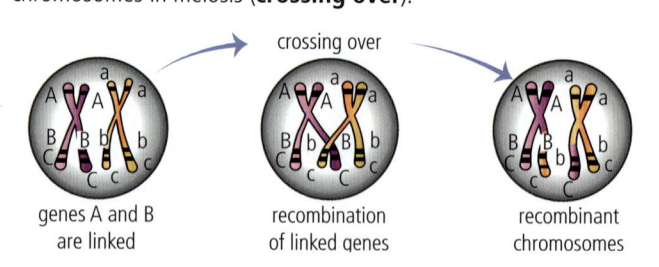

In accordance with the conclusions obtained from his experiments, Morgan proposed the ideas that would make up the **chromosomal theory of inheritance**:

- Genes are found on chromosomes.
- Genes are ordered in a linear fashion.

The recombination of genes that are located on the same chromosome is the result of chromosomal fragments being exchanged during the crossing over in meiosis.

ACTIVITIES

25. In your own words, briefly explain the concept of gene linkage.

6. Interpretation of Mendel's laws

> What types of gametes does an organism with genotype Aa produce?

The knowledge generated by the chromosomal theory of inheritance allows Mendelism to be better understood.

6.1 Current interpretation of Mendel's first law

In his experiments cross-pollinating different purebreds for their seed colours, Mendel used homozygotic individuals for each colour. All of the gametes produced from these parents were the same in terms of this trait. When the gametes were formed through meiosis, the homologous chromosomes separated and, therefore, so did the genes located on them.

Pure-breeding plants with yellow seeds have the **genotype AA** and, as a result, have two of the **same alleles**, one on each homologous chromosome. Therefore, all of the gametes that are created after meiosis carry the same type of allele: **A**.

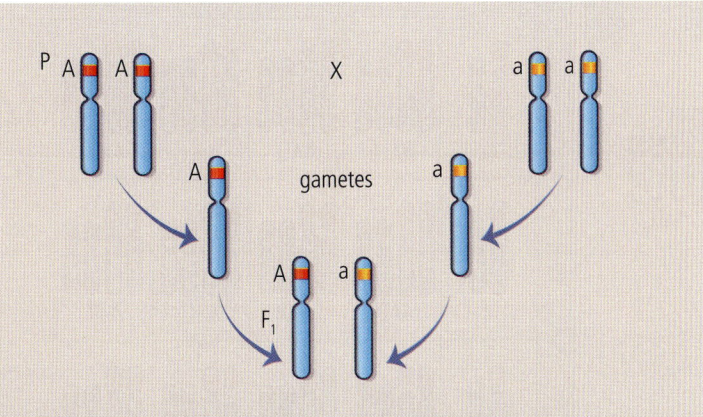

In the same way, pure-breeding plants with green seeds and the **genotype aa** produce gametes with the allele **a**.

Crossing involves the union of gametes carrying the A allele with gametes carrying the a allele, so all the offspring will be heterozygotic with the **genotype Aa**. All of them will have a yellow phenotype, because of the allele A being dominant over the allele a.

◯ By crossing two homozygotic individuals that differ in one trait, all of the offspring will be **heterozygotic** for that trait.

6.2 Current interpretation of Mendel's second law

Self-pollination of the F_1 generation with genotype Aa involves, firstly, meiosis and, subsequently, the formation of two types of gametes in equal amounts.

Half of the ova carry the allele **A**, and the other half the allele **a**.

The same happens with pollen. Half carry the allele **A**, and the other half the allele **a**.

The random union of the two types of pollen with the two types of ova produces the following genotypes and proportions in the F_2 generation: **1/4** are **AA**, **2/4** are **Aa** and **1/4** are **aa**.

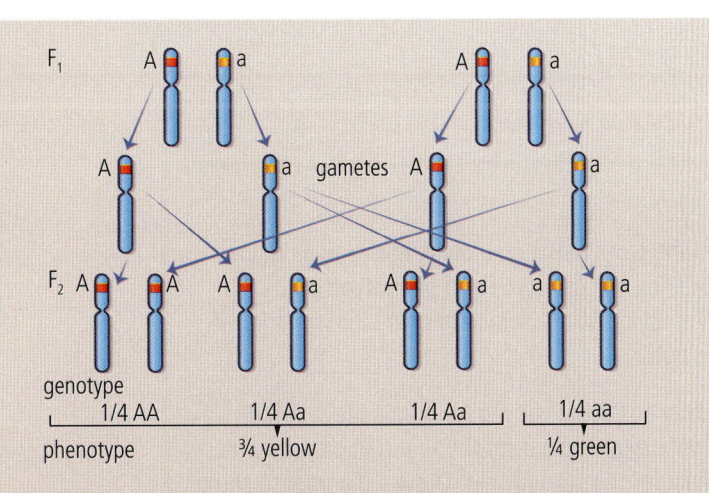

With regard to the **phenotype**, because of the dominant relationship, only 1/4 of the seeds will be green and the rest (3/4) will be yellow. Of the 3/4 that are yellow, 1/4 are homozygotic (AA), and 2/4 = 1/2 will be heterozygotic (Aa).

genotype: 1/4 AA | 1/4 Aa | 1/4 Aa | 1/4 aa
phenotype: ¾ yellow | ¼ green

◯ By crossing two heterozygotic individuals for a certain gene, half of the descendants will be heterozygotic, a quarter will be homozygotic for one allele, and another quarter will be homozygotic for the contrasting allele (**1/4, 2/4, 1/4**).

6.3 Current interpretation of Mendel's third law

To study the mechanism of inheritance for two different traits, Mendel crossed pure-breeding homozygotic dominant plants with round and yellow seeds (AALL) with homozygotic recessive plants with wrinkled and green seeds (aall).

1 Meiosis produces all the gametes of the dominant parent to be the same, with the genotype **AL**.

2 All of the gametes of the recessive parent are also the same and have the genotype **al**.

3 After fertilisation, all of the F_1 generation has the **same genotype AaLl**, and the **same phenotype**, round yellow seeds.

4 By leaving the F_1 generation to self-pollinate and then analysing this situation, it can be observed that the genotype **AaLl** creates four types of different gametes. This is because the genes for each trait are on different chromosomes. For this reason, both the pollen and the ova that are produced have the following possible genotypes: **AL**, **Al**, **aL** and **al**.

As can be seen, **four different phenotypes** can be observed in the proportions established by Mendel (9:3:3:1), along with nine **different genotypes** from combining the four alleles in all possible ways:

- round yellow seeds: AALL, AALl, AaLL, AaLl
- wrinkled yellow seeds: AAll, Aall
- round green seeds: aaLL, aaLl
- wrinkled green seeds: aall

5 By combining the four variants of gametes, nine different types of genotypes are produced. These are represented in what is called a **Punnet square**.

The genes that determine different traits are **transmitted independently** from generation to generation.

	AL	Al	aL	al
AL	AALL	AALl	AaLL	AaLl
Al	AALl	AAll	AaLl	Aall
aL	AaLL	AaLl	aaLL	aaLl
al	AaLl	Aall	aaLl	aall

ACTIVITIES

26. Draw a diagram to represent the cross between a black-haired male guinea pig and a female albino, indicating the genotype and phenotype of the parents until the F_2 generation. Black hair is dominant over albinism and the parents are purebred for this trait.

27. For garden pea plants, the axial position of flowers is dominant over the terminal flower position. A homozygotic plant for the first trait crosses with another homozygotic individual for the second trait. Draw a diagram to show the phenotype and genotype of the parents until the F_2 generation. Indicate the percentages of the genotypes and phenotypes obtained in the two filial generations.

6.4 Solving problems of Mendelian genetics

Solving problems regarding the traits that follow a Mendelian pattern of inheritance requires the information to be **suitably** organised.

To interpret these problems, the symbols or conventions used need to be known. Normally, the genotype of individuals is stated using letters, assigning a capital letter to the dominant allele and lower caps to the recessive allele.

MENDEL'S FIRST AND SECOND LAWS

For Mendel's first and second laws, pure-breeding parents for a certain trait are usually used, and the procedure indicated is repeated to study the outcome of the F_1 and F_2 generations.

1 The crossing of the parental genotypes is shown together with their sex to show the origin of the gametes involved.

2 The type of gametes provided by each parent is noted down.

3 All the possible combinations that can arise in fertilisation are established, avoiding unions between gametes coming from the same parent.

4 The different genotypes obtained in the offspring are shown, and their frequency is indicated in fractions or percentages.

5 The phenotypes for each genotype are given, along with their proportions, bearing in mind dominance, co-dominance or incomplete dominance between the different alleles.

6 If only the phenotype is known, all of the possible genotypes for that phenotype are noted.

	♂	X	♀
P phenotype	rough hair		smooth hair
genotype	AA		aa
gametes P	A A		a a
genotype	Aa		Aa
F_1 phenotype	rough hair (100%)		
	Aa		Aa
gametes F_1	A a		A a
genotype	AA	Aa Aa	aa
phenotype	3/4 rough hair		1/4 smooth hair

This diagram represents the cross between a rough-haired male guinea pig and a smooth-haired female, including the genotype and phenotype of the parents until the F_2 generation. The rough-haired trait is considered to be dominant over the smooth-haired trait and the parents are purebred for this trait.

ACTIVITIES

28. Draw a *Pisum sativum* cross between a heterozygotic individual for seed colour with another homozygotic recessive for the same trait. Interpret the results obtained.

MENDEL'S THIRD LAW

For Mendel's third law, pure-breeding parents for two different traits are usually used, and it is necessary to assume that these are determined by genes located on different chromosomes.

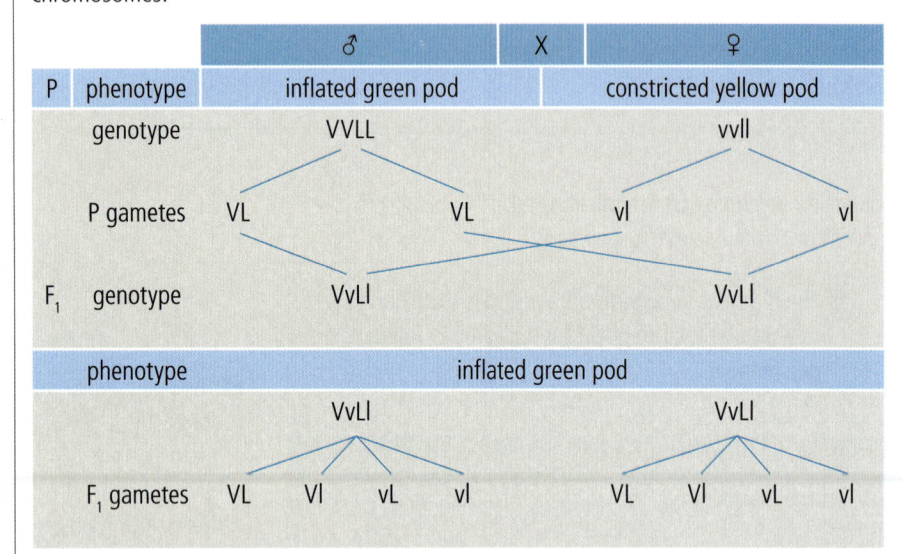

	♂	X	♀
P phenotype	inflated green pod		constricted yellow pod
genotype	VVLL		vvll
P gametes	VL VL		vl vl
F_1 genotype	VvLl		VvLl
phenotype		inflated green pod	
	VvLl		VvLl
F_1 gametes	VL Vl vL vl		VL Vl vL vl

	VL	Vl	vL	vl
VL	VVLL	VVLl	VvLL	VvLl
Vl	VVLl	VVll	VvLl	Vvll
vL	VvLL	VvLl	vvLL	vvLl
vl	VvLl	Vvll	vvLl	vvll

1 These are dealt with in the same way as problems **concerning** just one trait until the F_1 generation, **bearing in mind** that the two alleles for each trait separate to form the gametes.

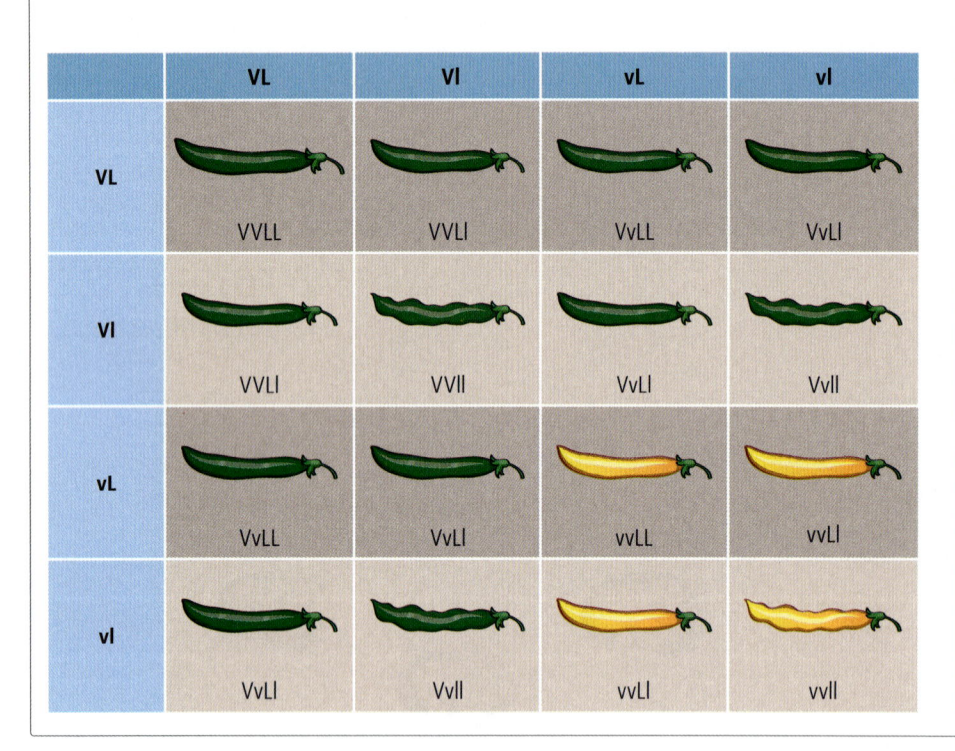

2 The four possible types of gametes produced by the F_1 generation are established by the combination of the two alleles of each trait.

3 Using a 4 × 4 Punnet square, the 16 genotypes generated in the F_2 generation are represented by the union of the four types of gametes provided by each sex of the F_1 generation.

4 The phenotypes corresponding to each genotype are obtained, along with their proportions, bearing in mind the relationships of dominance, co-dominance or incomplete dominance between the different alleles.

ACTIVITIES

29. In the garden pea plant, the trait for purple flowers is dominant over the trait for white flowers. A plant that is homozygotic for the first trait is crossed with another plant which is homozygotic for the second trait. Draw a diagram to show the phenotype and genotype of the parents until the F_2 generation. State the percentages and phenotypes obtained in the two filial generations.

30. In guinea pigs, the trait for rough hair is dominant over the trait for smooth hair. Also, the trait for black hair is dominant over the albino trait. Assuming that both traits depend on genes located on different chromosomes, establish the phenotypes, genotypes and percentages expected in the F_1 and F_2 generations if two pure-breeding parents, one with rough black hair and the other an albino with smooth hair, are crossed.

7. Human genetics

> Is the Rh factor dominant or recessive?

The Mendelian mechanisms of inheritance are also valid in humans. This allows us to determine the pattern for contrasting traits, such as sex or the most common blood groups in the population. It is of particular interest for providing information on different hereditary disorders or abnormalities, as their study and analysis can help their prevention.

7.1 Inheritance of human blood groups

The gene that determines blood groups in humans has many allelic variants, although the most common in our population are **A**, **B** and **0**. As each individual carries two alleles of each gene, the possible genotypes are **AA**, **BB**, **AB**, **A0**, **B0** and **00**.

The alleles A and B are dominant over the allele 0, but when A and B appear together, the relationship between them is one of **co-dominance**; this means that both manifest themselves at the same time. The phenotypes relating to each genotype are:

phenotype (blood group)	A	B	AB	O
genotype	AA, AO	BB, BO	AB	OO
antigens produced	A	B	A and B	no antigens
antibodies produced	anti-B	anti-A	none	anti-A and anti-B

Blood group A's erythrocytes have the A **antigen** protein on their plasma membrane. If they come into contact with blood from group B, they produce **antibodies** against the B antigen.

Blood group B has the B antigen and produces antibodies against the A antigen.

Blood group AB carries A and B antigens, which is why it does not manufacture antibodies against either type.

Blood group 0 has no antigens and therefore produces antibodies against A and B.

INHERITANCE OF THE BLOOD Rh FACTOR

The **Rhesus (Rh) factor** is a blood trait that clearly follows the Mendelian inheritance pattern. It concerns the presence of a protein, initially discovered in the blood of the rhesus monkey (*Macaca mulatta*), which also appears on the surface of erythrocytes of approximately 85% of humans. People who present this factor are called **Rh positives** (Rh+), while those who are lacking in it are **Rh negatives** (Rh−).

The Rh factor is dominant in terms of inheritance. The R allele dominates over the r, and its presence means that the surface of erythrocytes will contain the protein. The homozygotic RR and heterozygotic Rr genotypes have the Rh+ phenotype and the homozygotic rr genotypes have the Rh− phenotype.

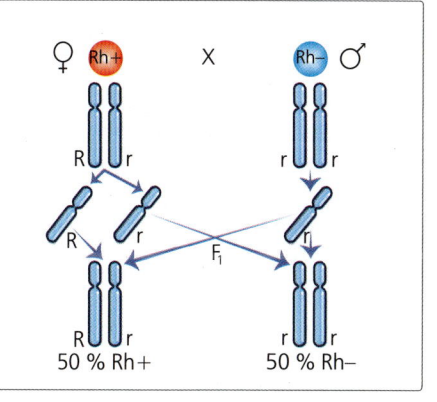

ACTIVITIES

31. Can a person with blood type O donate to anybody? Justify your answer.

32. If a man and a woman with blood type AB have children, could these children have blood type A? Could they have blood type O? Explain your answers.

33. Draw a diagram to represent the genotype and phenotype proportions of the descendants of two homozygotic individuals, one dominant and the other recessive, for the blood Rh factor.

7.2 Inheritance of sex

The inheritance of sex has many variants among living organisms. In some it depends on just one chromosome, while in others it is governed by just one gene, or several genes or environmental factors.

SEX DETERMINATION IN HUMANS

In humans, sex determination depends on the pair of **sex chromosomes**, which are represented by the letters **X** and **Y**. Unlike the rest of the pairs of homologous chromosomes (**autosomes**), the sex chromosomes X and Y are not very homologous: the Y chromosome is much smaller than the X chromosome. For this reason, they are also called **heterochromosomes**.

Women have the combination XX, and men have the combination XY. As a result of meiosis during female gametogenesis, when the chromosomal pairs separate, all the ova will carry an X chromosome, which is why women are known as the **homogametic sex**. On the other hand, in men, the disjunction of the pair of XY chromosomes causes half of the spermatozoa to carry an X and the other half, a Y, meaning that in the human species, the male is the **heterogametic sex**.

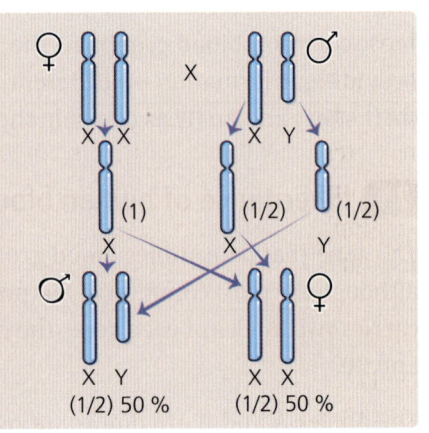

SEX-LINKED INHERITANCE

The human sex chromosomes X and Y are quite different in terms of size and genetic material. They have a small homologous area which allows them to pair up during meiosis. The genes on the non-homologous areas appear not to follow Mendel's laws, as generally the traits that they determine are only found on one of the sexes. For this reason, they are called **sex-linked traits**. Colour blindness and haemophilia are two genetic disorders linked to sex.

COLOUR BLINDNESS (DALTONISM)

This is a condition which prevents those affected from distinguishing between the colours red and green. It depends on recessive alleles of genes located on the non-homologous part of the X chromosome. In women, it is only expressed in homozygotes, but in men who carry the gene, it always expresses itself, as there is no allele on the Y chromosome to counteract it. This situation is known as **hemizygosis**.

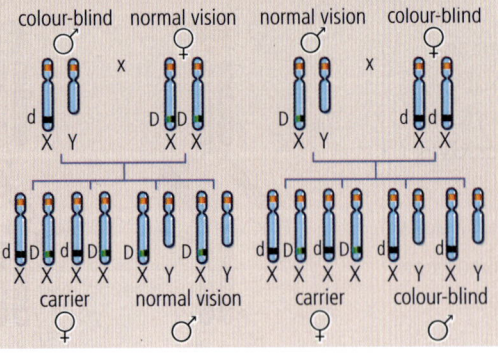

HAEMOPHILIA

Two of the three known types are sex-linked. Just like colour blindness, they depend on genes located on the non-homologous part of the X chromosome. Haemophilia consists of the inability of blood to clot on wounds. It rarely or never appears in women as for the disorder to manifest itself, two recessive alleles must be present.

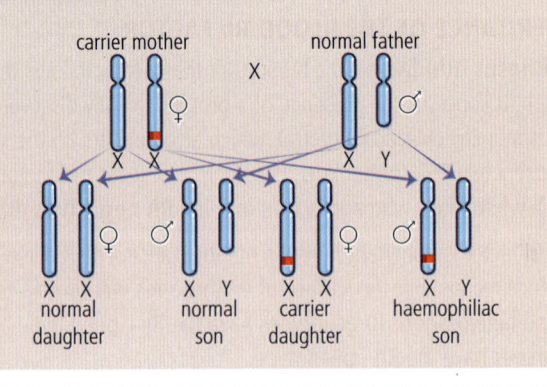

ACTIVITIES

34. Do you think that a person who does not suffer from haemophilia can transmit the disorder to their children? Justify your answer.

35. Research the history of haemophilia in European royal families and write a short report about it.

36. In humans, why is the number of births of girls almost practically the same as that of boys?

37. In a couple, the male has Rh negative blood and the female has Rh positive. If they had a child, what blood Rh factor would it have?

7.3 Solving problems of human genetics

To resolve these problems, the symbols or conventions used need to be known. When there are more than two allelic variants, different letters or numbers are used for each allele, such as the **AB0** system for blood groups. To study the Rhesus factor, the labels **Rh+** and **Rh−** are used in the phenotypes, and **R, r** for the dominant and recessive alleles, respectively. In questions of sex determination in humans, the letters **X** and **Y** are used to identify the sexual chromosomes. The same letter is also used for all the alleles and accompanied by a *subscript*, which indicates the variant. This is useful in representing sex-linked disorders due to genes on the X chromosome. Therefore, a defective recessive allele which causes haemophilia can be represented as X_h, or colour-blindness as X_d, compared with normal alleles, which are represented by **X**.

PRACTICAL APPLICATION OF BLOOD GROUP PROBLEMS

Indicate the frequency of phenotypes from the cross between a man with blood type A and a woman with blood type AB.

The woman's phenotype is AB; therefore, her genotype will be AB. The phenotype of the man is A, which is related to two possible genotypes: homozygotic (AA) or heterozygotic (A0). Therefore, the two potential situations are as follows:

AB WOMAN AND AA MAN

		♀	X	♂	
P	phenotype	AB		A	
	genotype	AB		AA	
	gametes	A B		A	
F_1	genotype	AA		AB	
		1/2		1/2	
		50%		50%	
	phenotype	A		AB	
		1/2		1/2	
		50%		50%	

○ Half of the children will have the genotype AA, and the other half the genotype AB. Therefore, in terms of their phenotype, half of the offspring will belong to blood group A, and the other half to blood group AB.

AB WOMAN AND A0 MAN

		♀		X		♂	
P	phenotype	AB				A	
	genotype	AB				A0	
	gametes	A	B			A	0
F_1	genotype	AA	A0			AB	B0
		1/4	1/4			1/4	1/4
		25%	25%			25%	25%
	phenotype	A				AB	B
		1/4 + 1/4 = 1/2				1/4	1/4
		50%				25%	25%

○ The genotypes AA, A0, AB and B0 are obtained with the same frequency, or rather, 1/4. In terms of their phenotype, half of the offspring will belong to blood group A and the other half will, in equal proportions, belong to blood groups AB and B.

ACTIVITIES

38. Indicate the frequencies of the genotypes and phenotypes expected in the children of a woman with blood type O and a man with blood type AB.

39. Indicate the frequencies of genotypes and phenotypes expected in the children of a woman with blood type A and a man with blood type B if both are heterozygotes.

PRACTICAL APPLICATION OF BLOOD Rh FACTOR PROBLEMS

Calculate the percentage of each genotype and phenotype which can arise from crossing two heterozygotic individuals for the human Rh factor.

As both are heterozygotes, the phenotype of the two individuals will be Rh+, and the genotype Rr, given that the inheritance of the human Rh factor is dominant.

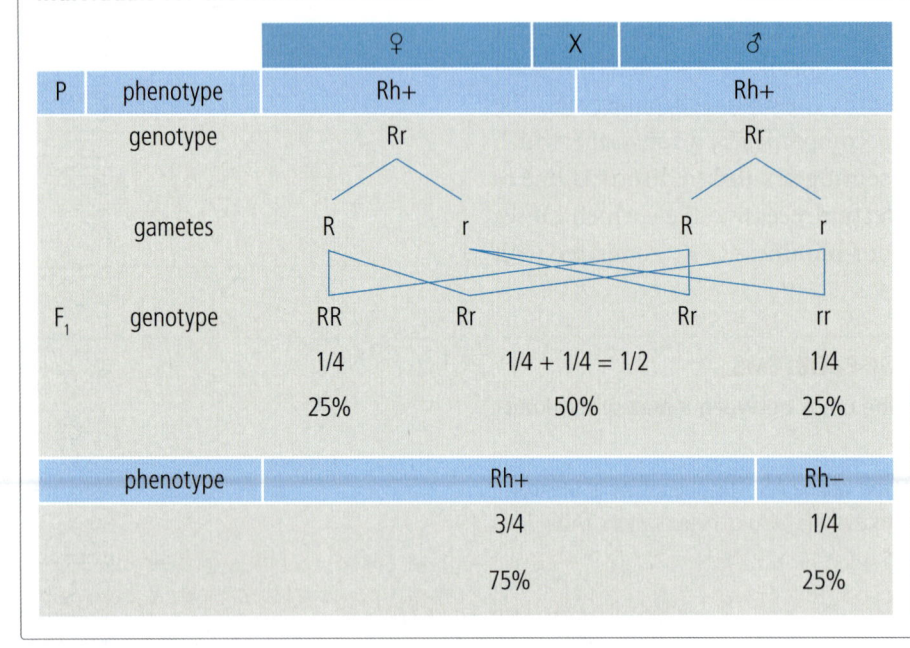

		♀	X		♂	
P	phenotype	Rh+			Rh+	
	genotype	Rr			Rr	
	gametes	R r			R r	
F_1	genotype	RR	Rr		Rr	rr
		1/4	1/4 + 1/4 = 1/2			1/4
		25%	50%			25%
	phenotype		Rh+		Rh−	
			3/4		1/4	
			75%		25%	

50% of the children will have the Rr genotype; 25% will have RR and the other 25% will have rr.

75% of the children will express the phenotype Rh+ and the remaining 25% will be Rh−.

PRACTICAL APPLICATION OF SEX-LINKED INHERITANCE PROBLEMS

Carry out a genetic study of the possible offspring that a man with one of the types of sex-linked haemophilia would have together with a woman who is not a carrier of the recessive allele.

The phenotype of the man will be as a sufferer of haemophilia, with the genotype X_hY, given that it is a recessive disorder due to the presence of the gene on the X chromosome and not on the Y chromosome. The woman will show no manifestation of the disorder and her genotype will be XX.

		♀	X		♂	
P	phenotype	normal			haemophilic	
	genotype	XX			X_hY	
	gametes	X X			X_h Y	
F_1	genotype	X_hX	X_hX		XY	XY
		1/2			1/2	
		50%			50%	
	phenotype	carrier			normal	
		1/2			1/2	
		50%			50%	

50% of the offspring will be male and will not have the disorder or carry the allele responsible.

50% of the offspring will be female and will not have the disorder but will be carriers of the defective allele.

ACTIVITIES

40. What is the percentage of each phenotype and genotype for the human blood Rh factor if a homozygotic individual is crossed with a heterozygotic individual?

41. Carry out a genetic study of the possible offspring that a man with one of the sex-linked types of haemophilia would have with a woman who was a carrier of the recessive allele.

Discovery techniques

SOLVING A TEST CROSS PROBLEM

> What is the test cross used for?

The **test cross** is a genetic analysis technique that is used to **differentiate between dominant homozygotic individuals and heterozygotic individuals** in terms of the same trait, as both express the same dominant phenotype. Although now these individuals can be differentiated by modern genetic engineering techniques, Mendel and his followers used it to distinguish between individuals with the same phenotype but different genotypes.

The **test cross** consists of crossing individuals whose genotype is unknown with organisms with a homozygotic recessive trait.

The term *backcross* or the adjective *back* is sometimes used to refer to this type of cross. This is because Mendel and his re-discoverers used to cross back the homozygous parent for the recessive trait to differentiate between heterozygotes and homozygotes in the F_2 generation.

The steps to follow are detailed below:

1. An individual of an unknown genotype and dominant phenotype is crossed with a homozygous recessive individual.
2. The gametes provided by each parent are noted.
3. The phenotypes of the offspring are examined. Two cases may occur:

PRACTICAL APPLICATION OF THE TEST CROSS

From crossing peas with yellow seeds and an unknown genotype with green seeds, we obtain offspring that is only formed of individuals with yellow seeds. What is the genotype of the seeds that have been crossed?

We know the genotype of the individuals with the green-seed phenotype (aa), but we do not know whether the genotype of the individuals with the yellow-seed phenotype is homozygotic dominant (AA) or heterozygotic (Aa).

As 100% of the offspring has the dominant phenotype, the genotype of the unknown parent is homozygotic (AA).

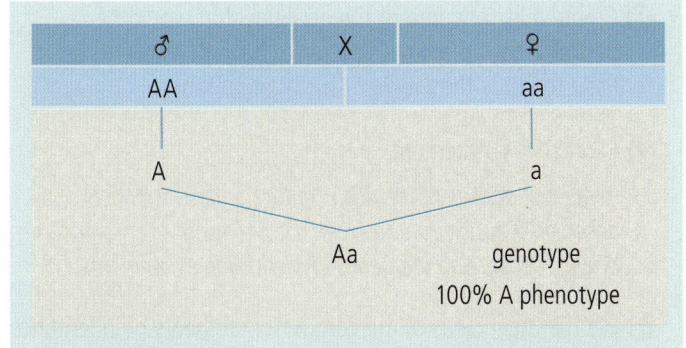

♂	X	♀
AA		aa
A		a

Aa genotype
100% A phenotype

If all the individuals obtained are of the dominant phenotype, it means that the unknown individual is a homozygote.

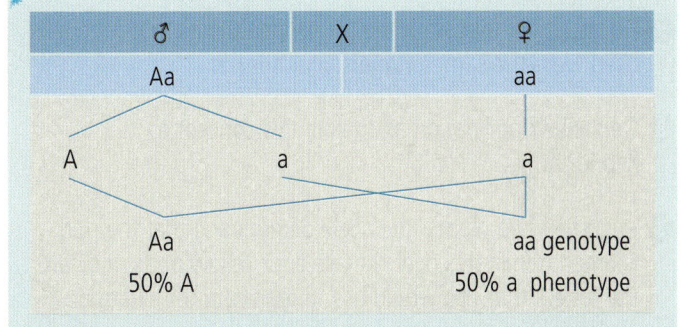

♂	X	♀
Aa		aa
A a		a

Aa — aa genotype
50% A — 50% a phenotype

If half of the individuals obtained are of the dominant phenotype and the other half show the recessive trait, the unknown individual is a heterozygote.

ACTIVITIES

1. Tall stalk length of the garden pea plant is dominant over short stalks. A plant with a tall stalk is pollinated with pollen from a short-stalked plant. All of the seeds obtained are sown, and half of the plants have tall stalks and the other half short stalks. With this data, indicate the genotype of the parents and the offspring.

2. Indicate the genotype of the parents and that of the offspring in the previous exercise if all of the F_1 plants have tall stalks.

3. Would you use a test cross to find out the genotype responsible for the colour of the flowers on the four o'clock flower plant (*Mirabilis jalapa*)? Why or why not?

Revision activities

1. Hugo de Vries (1848–1935), Carl Correns (1864–1933) and Erick von Tschermak (1871–1962) independently came to the same conclusions as Mendel with other species. Search for information in different resources on the rediscovery of Mendel's laws by these authors.

2. Explain the importance of the hereditary factors proposed by Mendel for the development of genetics. What is the name currently given to these factors?

3. What are allelomorphic genes?

4. Search for examples that help to understand the Mendelian concepts of purebreds and hybrids, and indicate what these types of individuals are currently called.

5. Briefly state Mendel's laws, giving an example from the animal kingdom.

6. State the phenotype of the F_1 generation from the cross of pure-breeding plants with inflated pods and plants with constricted pods.

7. Do you think that all of the yellow pea plants that Mendel used were the same? Explain your answer.

8. Define self-pollination and relate this concept to hybridisation.

9. In garden pea plants, the allele determining that the pod is green dominates over the allele for yellow pods. Indicate the letters that you would use to represent this situation and write the possible genotypes and their corresponding phenotypes.

10. Knowing that in humans a curved thumb is dominant over a straight thumb, indicate the genotypes corresponding to these two phenotypes with pairs of the letter c, using capital letters and lower caps.

11. Imagine an Andalusian chicken cross between a white-feathered parent and another bluish-grey-feathered parent. Indicate the proportions of the genotypes and phenotypes in the F_2 generation.

12. Revise and reproduce the diagram of meiosis. Draw a pair of alleles, A and a, on the chromosomes.

13. By cross-pollinating plants with white flowers with plants with purple flowers, an F_1 generation was obtained in which all of the offspring had purple flowers. By leaving the F_1 generation to self-pollinate, an F_2 generation of 693 plants with purple flowers and 231 with white flowers was obtained. Interpret the results of the F_1 and F_2 generations with the corresponding Mendelian law.

14. Mendel cross-pollinated pure-breeding garden pea plants for their pod and seed colour. He pollinated plants with yellow pods and green seeds with the pollen from plants with green pods and yellow seeds. Bearing in mind the dominance of these two traits, indicate the possible genotypes and phenotypes and the expected frequency of each in the F_1 and F_2 generations.

15. Flower colour for the four o'clock flower is a trait with incomplete dominance. The flowers can be red or white, and those of the hybrid are pink. Indicate the genotype and phenotype proportions which would arise from crossing a plant with white flowers with another with pink flowers.

16. Create a list of some of the qualities that would be desirable for an animal species to have if it were to be used to study the mechanisms of inheritance.

17. Explain this statement:

    In the first decade of the 20th century, various scientists observed a parallelism between the behaviour of chromosomes during meiosis and the genes in Mendelian experiments.

18. List the main ideas of the chromosomal theory of inheritance and explain what this theory means for Mendelism.

19. Bearing in mind Laplace's rule, calculate the following:
    a. The probability that the spermatozoa of a man will carry the Y chromosome.
    b. The probability that the ova of a woman will carry the X chromosome.
    c. The probability that the spermatozoa of a man will carry the X chromosome.

20. The trait for curly hair in dogs is dominant over the trait for straight hair. Two curly-haired dogs have a curly-haired puppy. To know whether it is heterozygotic, what type of female would it have to be crossed with? Why?

21. Calculate the percentage of each genotype and each phenotype that is expected in the offspring of a heterozygotic individual with the Rh factor and another homozygotic dominant individual with the same trait.

22 Interpret Morgan's illustration of the cross between normal females with red eyes and males with white eyes of the species *Drosophila melanogaster*.

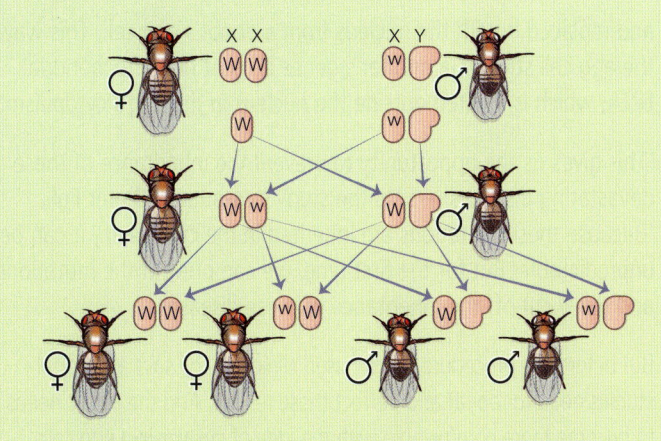

23 With the aid of the illustration, explain what is meant by the genes B and C presenting greater linkage than A and B or A and C.

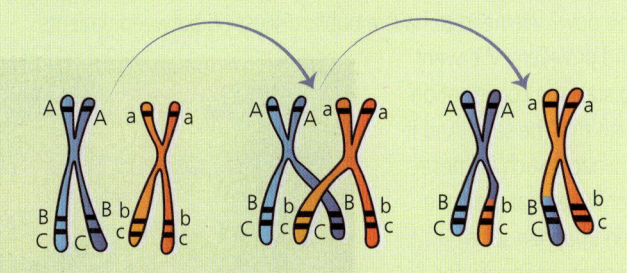

24 Indicate the genotype and phenotype proportions of the offspring of a colour-blind woman with a man not suffering from this condition.

25 Copy the following table into your notebook and fill it in with a + or − sign depending on whether the recipient presents an immunological reaction.

recipient	donor			
	A	B	AB	0
A				
B				
AB				
0				

26 Briefly research the history of blood transfusions and how blood groups were discovered.

27 Indicate the genotype and phenotype frequencies of the children of type A and type B parents if both are homozygotic for this trait.

28 Can a homozygote with blood type A donate blood to someone with type 0? And if the donor were a heterozygote?

29 In humans, the albino trait is determined by a recessive gene that is not linked to sex. A dark-haired woman whose father is albino wants to have children with another dark-haired man who does not have a history of albinism in his family. Could they still have an albino child? Explain your answer.

30 Search various resources for information on hereditary human disorders and write a short report on their characteristics and the most frequent types.

31 Indicate which of the following statements are incorrect and correct them.
   a. By crossing two heterozygotic individuals that have a contrasting trait, all the offspring will be homozygotic for that trait.
   b. The genes that determine different traits are transmitted independently from generation to generation.
   c. People that belong to blood group A have the genotype AA.
   d. The inheritance of sex in living organisms depends on a single chromosome.
   e. Haemophilia is a disorder that is always linked to sex.

32 Clarify the concept of a test cross with the aid of an example.

33 Search various resources for information on the incompatibility of Rh in pregnant mothers with Rh− phenotype.

34 In the *Pisum sativum* species, the inheritance of sex has not been studied. What do you think is the reason for this?

35 A couple has five boys. The mother is pregnant again. What is the probability of her having a girl? Explain your answer.

36 State the genotype and phenotype proportions in the offspring of a woman and a colour-blind man.

37 Calculate the genotype and phenotype proportions expected in a woman who is a carrier of the recessive allele for haemophilia and a man who does not suffer from haemophilia.

38 Can a man pass on haemophilia to his sons? Can he pass it on to his daughters? Explain your answers with a diagram.

39 People with blood type O that is Rh− receive the name of 'universal donors'. Why do you think this is?

UNIT 03 The inheritance of traits

Read and think

NEW TECHNIQUE TO PREVENT CERTAIN INHERITED DISEASES

Passing on genetic mutations for disease is one of the greatest fears among parents-to-be, but a new technique may **alleviate** some of those worries.

Mitochondrial disorders affect about 1 in 10 000 people and can cause a range of medical problems from **stunted** growth, vision loss, and neurological disorders to kidney disease. Some of these originate in mutations that code for mitochondria, which are the cell's **workhorses** that **churn out** the energy a cell needs in order to function. Other aberrations can arise from mitochondria's own DNA; mitochondria hold a unique place in human biology because they contain their own unique DNA and can make their own proteins, apart from the proteins that the cell manufactures.

Currently, there are no cures for mitochondrial disorders, many of which are passed from mother to child since children inherit their mother's mitochondrial DNA from the egg. Symptoms of these conditions typically appear in childhood, and women who carry such mutations often have to choose between not having children or undergoing in vitro fertilisation (IVF) with donor eggs in order to avoid passing on a genetic condition.

However, researchers from New York may have found a way to prevent inheritance of these disorders with a technique that involves transferring a cell's nucleus, and not its mitochondrial DNA, into a different human egg containing healthy mitochondria.

The research is published in the journal *Nature* and describes how the team successfully removed the nucleus of an unfertilized egg and replaced it with the nucleus from a donor's egg cell. This way, the egg cell still has a mother's genes but not her mitochondrial DNA, which is located outside the nucleus in the egg's cytoplasm.

'This gives us the opportunity to prevent the inheritance of these devastating diseases' – says the study's co-author, Dieter Egli. 'Because these mutations are inherited in the cytoplasm, it can be unpredictable. But for the first time, we can prevent the mutations and really cut off the inheritance of these diseases.'

But before the procedure can be used clinically, Egli says additional studies need to repeat and perfect these results. And the public needs to become more comfortable with the idea of **swapping** egg cells, something that may still be too much of a social and ethical **hurdle** for many. 'I think to a large extent, the greatest challenge ahead is the opinion of people. Can we convince people that we should be doing this now? We need to have a public discussion between patients and providers. We want to start the conversation with this,' he says. And if advances such as these continue, that dialogue can't happen soon enough, especially for families who are affected by mitochondrial disorders.

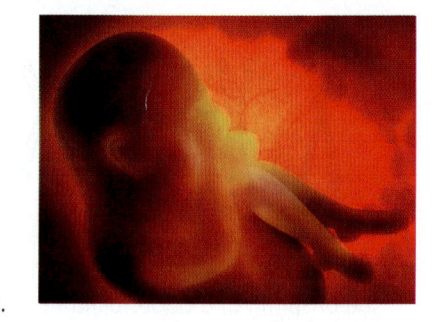

Adapted from an article published by Alexandra Sifferlin in *Time* on 3 January, 2013

ANSWER THE QUESTIONS

1. What two types of mutations can cause mitochondrial disorders?
2. Search the text for symptoms attributed to mitochondrial inherited diseases. How common are they?
3. From what you have learnt in this unit, what is an inherited disease? Would mitochondrial disorders be considered inherited diseases?
4. According to the information provided in the text, how do you think mitochondrial disorders are treated?
5. According to what you have learnt in this unit, what kind of inheritance would mitochondrial disorders caused by mutations in mitochondrial DNA follow?
6. Look up which hereditary disease is the most common in Spain. What does it involve, and what kind of inheritance does it show?
7. The article mentions ethical concerns related to this potential cure of mitochondrial disorders. It has even been suggested that children born after this therapy is applied would have three 'parents' (the father; the mother, who would provide her egg's nuclear DNA; and a second mother, who would provide the rest of the egg). Split the class into two groups and debate the ethical advantages and disadvantages of this new technique.

Work it out

CONCEPT MAP

Use the words in the word cloud to create your own unit map in your notebook. Write any connecting texts you need.

genes
the inheritance of traits
reinterpretation of Mendel's laws
Thomas Hunt Morgan
gene linkage
hereditary factors
recombination and crossing over
the chromosomal theory of inheritance
sex
sex-linked conditions
human blood groups
Gregor Mendel
Genetics
Mendel's laws
human genetics
incomplete dominance

SELF-ASSESSMENT

Carry out a self-assessment of what you learned in this unit. Choose one answer for each question and then check your answers.

1 The dominant allele ...
   a. never manifests itself.
   b. only manifests itself in absence of the recessive allele.
   c. always manifests itself.

2 What is the correct order for Mendel's experiments?
   a. P generation cross-pollination, filial self-pollination, result interpretation
   b. P generation self-pollination, filial cross-pollination, result interpretation
   c. P generation self-pollination, result interpretation, filial cross-pollination

3 Recessive traits hidden in the F_1 generation appearing again in the F_2 generation in the proportion of three dominants for every recessive is ...
   a. Mendel's first law.
   b. Mendel's second law.
   c. Mendel's third law.

4 According to Mendel, what is the F_2 ratio for two independent traits?
   a. 4:4:4:4
   b. 6:6:2:2
   c. 9:3:3:1

5 Incomplete dominance causes ...
   a. trait hybridisation.
   b. violation of Laplace's rule.
   c. heterogeneous P generations.

6 What explains genes in the same chromosome behaving as non-linked?
   a. Separation of chromosomes in gametes
   b. Chromosome alignment during meiosis
   c. Recombination of chromatids

7 How many different genotypes are possible for two independent traits?
   a. 9
   b. 4
   c. 2

8 What is the name of the diagram used to predict the outcome of a genetic cross?
   a. A Bateson square
   b. A Punnet square
   c. A Correns square

9 A person with blood type AB+ is a ...
   a. universal donor.
   b. universal recipient.
   c. donor for groups A, B and AB.
   d. recipient of both positive and negative rhesus groups 0, A, B and AB.

10 What is it called when a gene in the X chromosome does not have a corresponding allele on the Y chromosome?
   a. Heterogamesis
   b. Haemophilia
   c. Hemizygosis

04 Molecular genetics

<<LOOKING BACK

- What is DNA and where can it be found?
- What do you think the science of genetic engineering studies?
- Why is Dolly the sheep famous?
- What are stem cells used for? Where do they come from?
- What is biotechnology?
- Is it possible to get blue strawberries? Why or why not? What do you think their advantages could be?

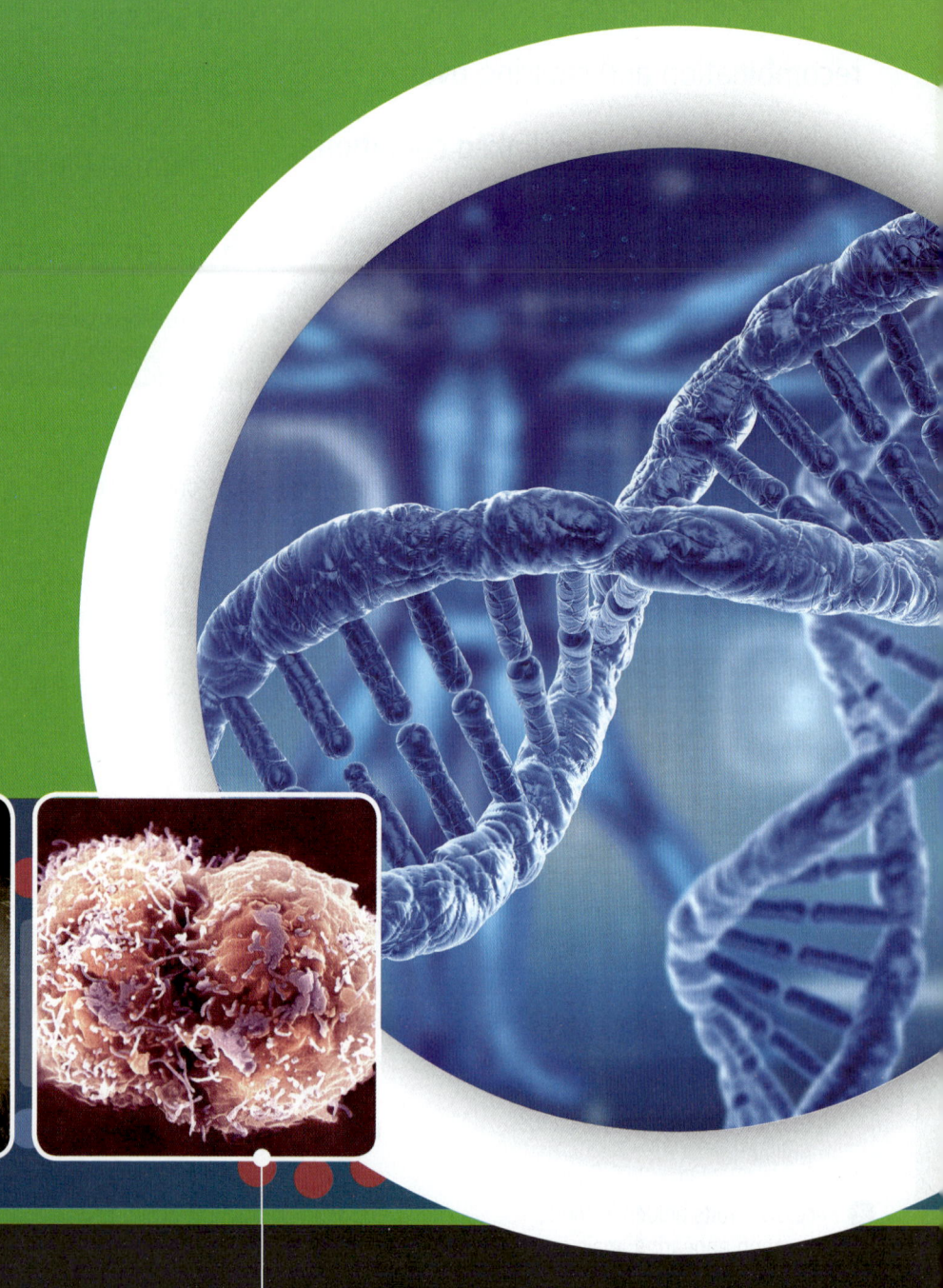

Dolly the sheep

Mammalian stem cells

Fluorescent pets?

In 2007, South Korean scientists created glow-in-the-dark cats. They altered the DNA of a donor cat's skin cells using a virus, transplanted the cells into the ova, and implanted the ova back into the cat's womb ... and her kittens were fluorescent!

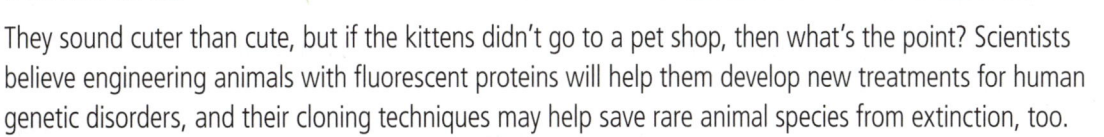

They sound cuter than cute, but if the kittens didn't go to a pet shop, then what's the point? Scientists believe engineering animals with fluorescent proteins will help them develop new treatments for human genetic disorders, and their cloning techniques may help save rare animal species from extinction, too.

Altering an organism's DNA or combining it with other DNA to create new genes sounds like science fiction, but genetically modified organisms are an increasing part of our modern life. There are goats that produce silk instead of milk, venom-producing cabbages and cows that help reduce the greenhouse effect. The next time you need a vaccine, the doctor might just give you a genetically modified banana instead of an injection!

- What is a genetically modified organism?
- What is a clone? What was the first cloned animal?
- There are ethical issues in genetic engineering. Why is that? What issues are there?
- Do you think genetic engineering is acceptable or not? Why?

LOOKING FORWARD >>

- What makes DNA molecules highly stable?
- What is the difference between the processes of transcription and translation?
- What is a nullisomy?
- What is *in situ* hybridisation used for?
- What is the controversy over biotechnology?
- What are the steps in the polymerase chain reaction?
- How can we determine the polypeptide corresponding to a DNA strand?

1 Nucleic acids

> **What makes DNA molecules highly stable?**

There are two types of nucleic acids: **deoxyribonucleic acid (DNA)**, which together with associated proteins makes up chromatin and nuclear chromosomes, and **ribonucleic acid (RNA)**, which is present in both the nucleus and the cytoplasm, and performs various functions.

1.1 Deoxyribonucleic acid

In 1953, **James Watson** and **Francis Crick**, building on the research of **Maurice Wilkins**, **Rosalind Franklin** and **Raymond Gosling**, proposed a three-dimensional model for the structure of the DNA molecule.

In cells, there are molecules of DNA in the nucleus, the mitochondria and the chloroplasts.

Together they adopt a structure that resembles a spiral staircase, with the steps being the nitrogenous base pairs of each strand.

DNA is a **double helix** that coils to the right and is formed of two long chains or **complementary strands** of nucleotides.

The stability of the structure comes from the nitrogenous bases stacked in the centre of the double helix and the hydrogen bonds bridging the nitrogenous bases of both strands. There are two or three **hydrogen bonds** between the complementary nucleotide pairs.

The strands are **antiparallel**, meaning that one starts at one end of the double helix, while the accompanying strand starts at the other end.

The **nucleotides** are the units making up the long strands of nucleic acids. They are composed of a nitrogenous base, a sugar (**deoxyribose**) and at least one **phosphate group**.

In DNA, there are four types of nucleotides, depending on their **nitrogenous base**. The chemical properties of the nitrogenous bases only allow **adenine (A)** to be paired **with thymine (T)**, and **cytosine (C) with guanine (G)**.

ACTIVITIES

1. James Watson and Francis Crick received the Nobel Prize in Physiology or Medicine in 1962. Find out why they were awarded this prize.

1.2 Ribonucleic acid

In 1868, the Swiss doctor and biologist **Friedrich Miescher** (1844–1895) described ribonucleic acid (RNA), which he called nuclein.

It is found in both the nucleus and the cytoplasm, and is composed of a single strand of nucleotides. These nucleotides are the same as those making up deoxyribonucleic acid, except that the sugar is a ribose and thymine is replaced by **uracil** (U), another nitrogenous base with similar characteristics.

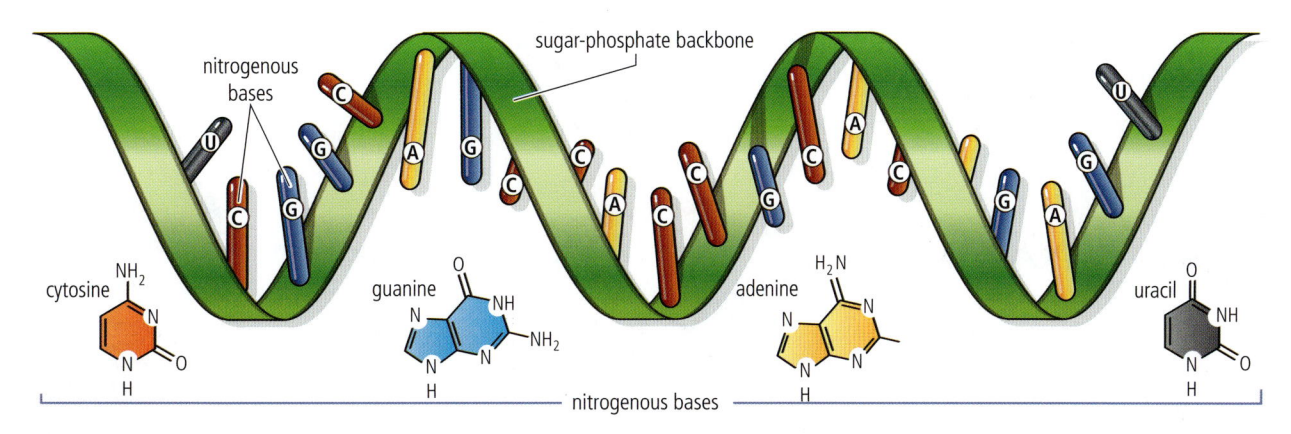

TYPES OF RNA

Depending on their location and function, there are three types of RNA:

- **Messenger RNA (mRNA)** is a copy of the DNA information; it transports the genetic information from the nucleus to the cytoplasm, where it acts as a **template** for protein synthesis.
- **Transfer RNA (tRNA)** is a small molecule responsible for transporting and adding the appropriate amino acid to the protein that is being synthesised.
- **Ribosomal RNA (rRNA)** combines with different proteins to form the structure of the ribosomes.

1.3 Differences between DNA and RNA

Although DNA and RNA molecules are similar, they do have some distinguishable features in terms of their composition and function.

	structure	sugar	nitrogenous bases	location	function
DNA	double helix coiling to the right	deoxyribose	adenine cytosine guanine thymine	nucleus mitochondria chloroplast	Stores and transmits genetic information.
RNA	simple strand	ribose	adenine cytosine guanine uracil	nucleus cytoplasm ribosome	Transports genetic information and uses it to synthesise proteins.

ACTIVITIES

2. What are the features that differentiate DNA from RNA in terms of their composition?

2. Functions of nucleic acids

> What is the difference between the processes of transcription and translation?

Once the structure of DNA was known and the idea that genes control protein synthesis was accepted, it was necessary to learn how this control was managed. The observation that nucleic acids and proteins are long polymers led on to the search for a relationship between the linear order of the nucleotides in the nucleic acids and the sequence of the amino acids in the proteins. This search brought about the establishment of the **central dogma** of molecular biology. This dogma explains that DNA codes for RNA, which codes for proteins.

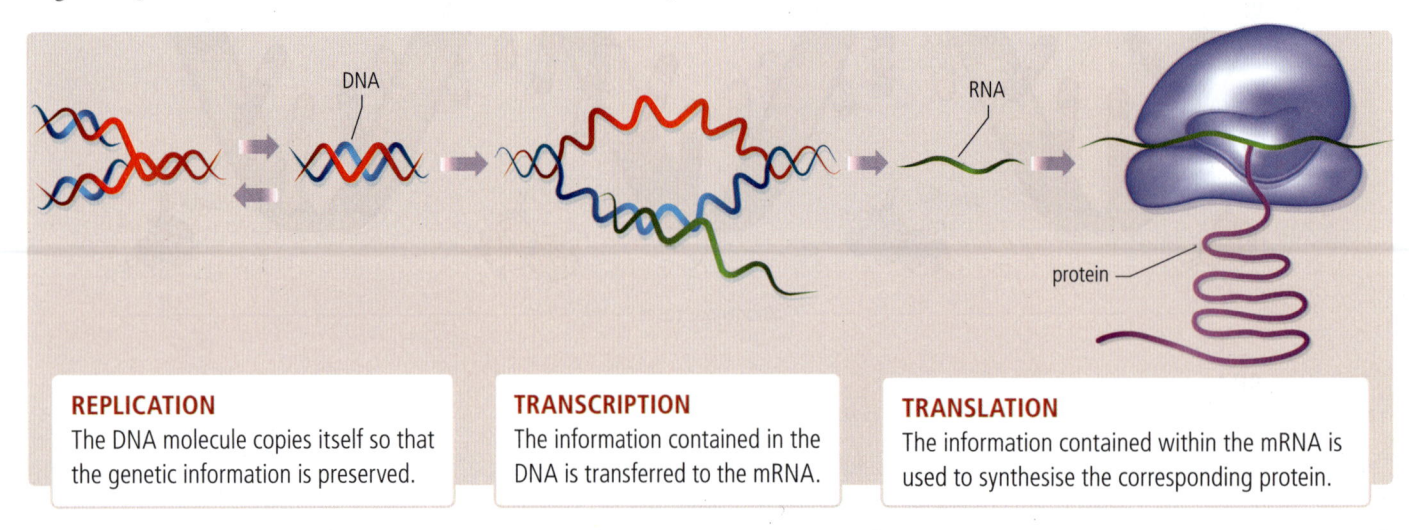

REPLICATION
The DNA molecule copies itself so that the genetic information is preserved.

TRANSCRIPTION
The information contained in the DNA is transferred to the mRNA.

TRANSLATION
The information contained within the mRNA is used to synthesise the corresponding protein.

2.1 Replication

Replication is the process by which DNA can form identical copies of itself. The two strands making up the DNA represent a pair of **complementary templates** in which, opposite an A, there would be a T, and opposite a C, there would be a G. Each strand can separate from its complementary pair and act as a template to synthesise a new complementary strand.

Both the separation of the complementary strands of the original DNA molecule and the joining of nucleotides to form new strands are processes which are catalysed by specific enzymes. These include **DNA polymerases**, also known as **replicases**.

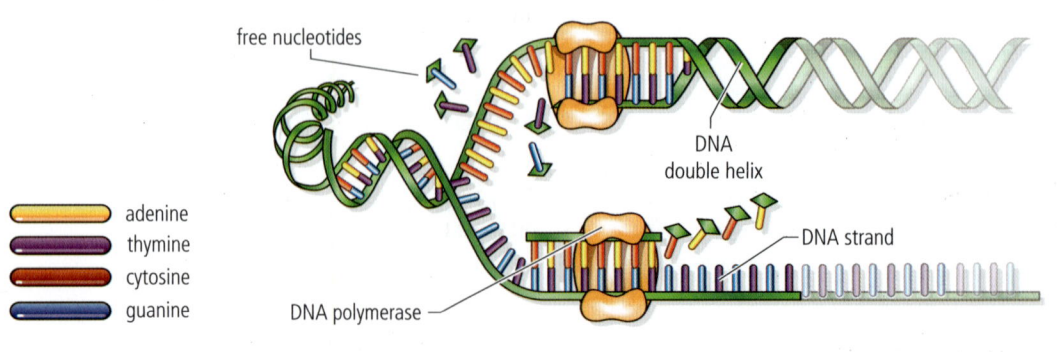

1. Specialised **enzymes** separate the two chains of DNA which will act as templates.

2. The replicases add complementary nucleotides to the strand acting as a template.

3. **Two new molecules of DNA** appear, each with two strands. One of the strands from each molecule comes from the original molecule, while the other strand has been newly synthesised.

2.2 Transcription

Transcription is the process in which the information contained in the DNA is transferred as mRNA. This is how the genetic information leaves the nucleus.

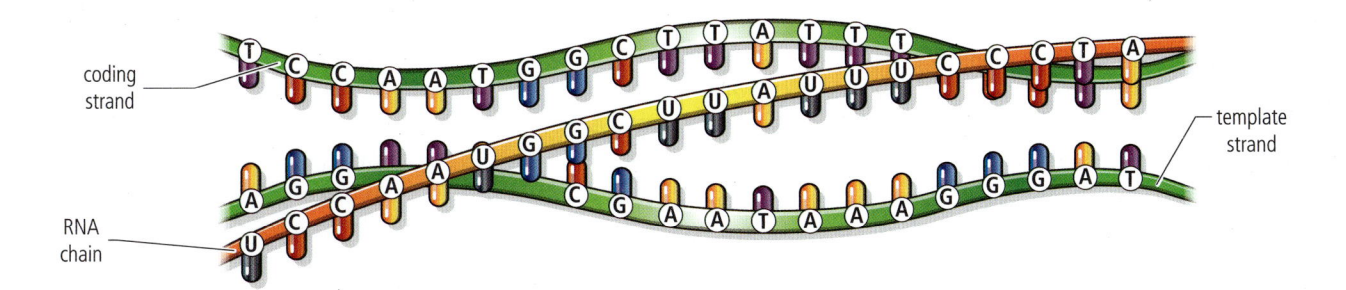

coding strand

template strand

RNA chain

1 The two DNA strands separate. The strand that is going to be copied is called the **template strand**. Its complementary pair is the **coding strand**; its sequence of bases is the same as that of the mRNA.

2 **RNA polymerases** or **transcriptases** add nucleotides to the new RNA chain.

3 Once the mRNA has been transcribed, this separates and the two strands of DNA join back up again.

ACTIVITIES

3. Search for information on the events that made the establishment of the central dogma of molecular biology possible, and say which scientist defended it. Write a report with any information you obtain.

4. One of the strands of a certain molecule of DNA presents the base sequence AAAGCGCTAGC. State the sequence of the complementary strand.

5. Draw a diagram to represent the replication of a segment of DNA that has the sequence AAAGCGCTAGC on one of its strands. Indicate which strand comes from the original molecule and which has been newly formed in the two molecules at the end.

6. What is the difference between a replicase and a transcriptase?

7. The following sequence relates to the first nucleotides on a gene. Knowing that the top strand is the coding strand and that transcription occurs from left to right, state the sequence of the mRNA fragment that is transcribed from this DNA.

    ATGGCATTAGACCTATAT
    TACCGTAATCTGGATATA

8. The following sequences relate to single strands of nucleic acids. Say whether they are RNA or DNA strands, and explain the criteria that you have used for your classification.

    a. AUGGGGAAACGUUAUUUU
    b. TTTCGCGAATTAAACGCG
    c. AGCCCCGCAAGGCCCAAG
    d. CTCGGTGATAAGCTGTCC
    e. CTCGGTGATAAGCTGTCC
    f. UGGAACCCCUUUU

BIG THINKER

Barbara McClintock was a scientist during a period when women were expected to be housewives, but she became the most distinguished cytogeneticist in history. While a researcher at Cornell University, a colleague attributed more than half her department's important discoveries between 1929 and 1935 to McClintock alone. In the 1940s and 50s, she discovered 'jumping genes', mobile genetic elements, and was awarded a Nobel Prize for this breakthrough in 1983. Science was only one of her interests: she enjoyed swimming, skating, and playing volleyball and tennis (but not at the same time!). Does that sound like a good work/life balance?

UNIT 04 Molecular genetics

GENETIC CODE

In nucleic acids, information is written in a language consisting of four letters, in accordance with the nitrogenous bases of the nucleotides: A, G, C and T in DNA and A, G, C and U in RNA. In terms of human proteins, the language contains 20 letters corresponding to the 20 essential amino acids that make up their sequence. Translating the language based on four letters to one based on 20 is possible through groups of three bases known as **codons** or **triplets**, which code for specific amino acids. With four letters, they can be arranged in $4^3 = 64$ different triplets, which are the keys to the **genetic code**. As there are 20 amino acids, the majority of them have various codes. This phenomenon is called **synonymy**.

The following table shows which amino acid is represented by each codon. Therefore, the triplet UGG in mRNA is tryptophan in the protein. The codon **AUG** of methionine is also the codon that starts the synthesis of the protein. The codons **UAA**, **UAG** and **UGA** are signs punctuating the end of the translation.

		SECOND LETTER				
		U	C	A	G	
FIRST LETTER	U	UUU, UUC phenylalanine; UUA, UUG leucine	UCU, UCC, UCA, UCG serine	UAU, UAC tyrosine; UAA, UAG stop	UGU, UGC cysteine; UGA stop; UGG tryptophan	U C A G (THIRD LETTER)
	C	CUU, CUC, CUA, CUG leucine	CCU, CCC, CCA, CCG proline	CAU, CAC histidine; CAA, CAG glutamine	CGU, CGC, CGA, CGG arginine	U C A G
	A	AUU, AUC, AUA isoleucine; AUG methionine	ACU, ACC, ACA, ACG threonine	AAU, AAC asparagine; AAA, AAG lysine	AGU, AGC serine; AGA, AGG arginine	U C A G
	G	GUU, GUC, GUA, GUG valine	GCU, GCC, GCA, GCG alanine	GAU, GAC aspartic acid; GAA, GAG glutamic acid	GGU, GGC, GGA, GGG glycine	U C A G

A UNIVERSAL CODE

One of the most significant features of the genetic code is that it is **universal**. This means that the same codon codes for the same amino acid in all living organisms, whether it is an algae or a reptile. This fact is one of the most significant pieces of evidence for a **single origin of life**.

This code also allows techniques such as **recombinant DNA** with human DNA to be used, which can be expressed in an organism as distant, evolutionarily speaking, as bacteria.

ACTIVITIES

9. Write the DNA nucleotide sequence that comes from the following mRNA sequence: AUGAAUAACUGUAGUUCUCCGUGA. Which is the coding strand? Which is the template strand?

10. Find the genetic code for the codon of the amino acid leucine in the table. What else do you find? Explain your answer.

11. Indicate which amino acid relates to the following codons:
    a. UGA
    b. UAU
    c. UUU
    d. CCC
    e. CCA

2.3 Translation

Translation is the process which enables a protein to be synthesised in ribosomes from the message transcribed in the mRNA.

In the language of genetic code, the sequence of mRNA bases is read from a certain point, without a gap between codons. The bases are not used twice either, meaning that a base can only belong to one codon.

The amino acids making up the different proteins are dispersed in the cytoplasm and join together through covalent bonds in the order indicated in the mRNA.

> **NEW DEFINITION OF GENE**
>
> Knowledge of molecular genetics allowed Mendel's hereditary factors to be redefined. Genes are now understood to be a segment of DNA formed of a sequence of nucleotides, which determine the proper sequencing of the amino acids of a **polypeptide**.

1 mRNA is joined to ribosomes at the appropriate end, starting translation.

The attachment of the corresponding amino acid to each codon in the ribosomes occurs with the help of **tRNA**.

The tRNA molecules are specific to each amino acid and have a central area of three complementary bases for each mRNA codon. This area is called the **anticodon**.

2 The ribosome moves along the mRNA, and the tRNA successively pairs up with the appropriate amino acids for each mRNA codon, thanks to the **complementarity** of the anticodon.

3 Gradually, each new amino acid is added to the growing protein.

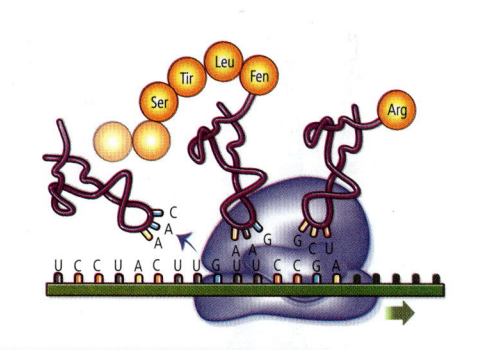

4 A tRNA molecule repeatedly arrives at the ribosome carrying an amino acid and leaves without it. The ribosome continues moving along the mRNA until it reaches one of the codons, signalling a **stop** (UUA, UAG or UGA). As there is no tRNA to recognise it, protein synthesis has finished.

ACTIVITIES

12. What sequence of amino acids corresponds with the following sequence of nucleotides on an mRNA molecule if the translation is carried out from left to right?

AUGAAUAACUGUAGUUCUCCGUGA

13. In addition to messenger RNA (mRNA) and transfer RNA (tRNA), there is ribosomal RNA (rRNA). Research them all and present the similarities and differences between these three types of RNA in a table.

14. Compare the processes of replication, transcription and translation.

3. Mutations

> **What is a nullisomy?**

Mutations are alterations in the genetic material that have negative, positive or no consequences at all for the living organisms in which they occur. They are due to errors in DNA replication or abnormal distributions in cell divisions. They can be chromosome or gene mutations, depending on where they occur.

CHROMOSOME MUTATIONS

These are alterations which affect large segments of chromosomes or entire chromosomes and, therefore, many genes. They can be structural or numerical.

STRUCTURAL MUTATIONS

These are due to the appearance of two breakages in nuclear chromosomes at the same time. In these circumstances, the four broken ends can join up again in any other possible combination, which produces different mutations:

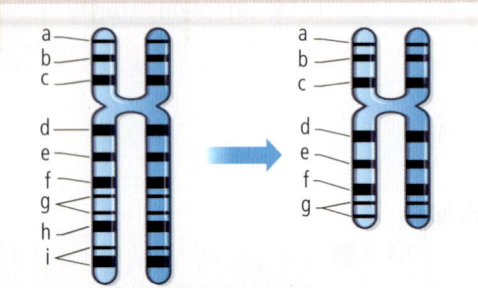

Deletion is the loss of a chromosomal segment as a result of two **breakages** that occur on the same chromosome and the disappearance of the middle segment.

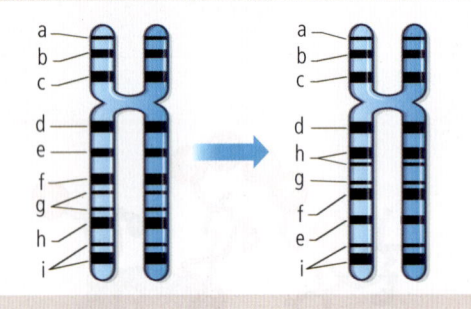

Inversion is the change in direction of the chromosomal segments, due to two breakages on the same chromosome and the segment's re-joining the wrong way round.

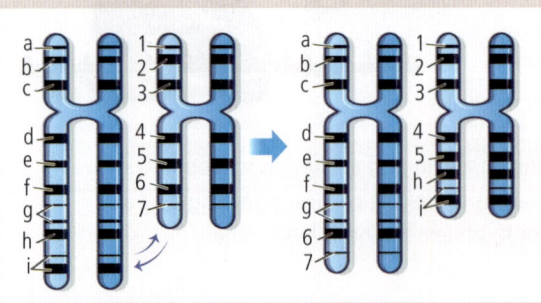

Translocation is caused when a segment splits off from a chromosome and exchanges with the segment of a non-homologous chromosome.

NUMERICAL MUTATIONS

These affect the normal number of chromosomes of a species without affecting their structure.

There are different types of numerical mutations that affect individual chromosomes:

- **Nullisomy** appears when a pair of homologous chromosomes is missing in an organism.
- **Monosomy** occurs when a chromosome is missing from each of the homologous pairs.
- **Trisomy** is the existence of an extra chromosome in a pair of homologous chromosomes.

Other mutations affect the entire set of chromosomes:

- **Haploidy** occurs when the number of chromosomes in an organism matches the number of gametes for its species.
- **Polyploidy** occurs when an organism presents more than two complete sets of chromosomes. If the organism has three sets, it is **triploid**; if it has four, it is **tetraploid**, etc. If the chromosomal sets are all derived from the same species, the condition is called **autopolyploidy**; if they come from different species, it is known as **allopolyploidy**.

GENE MUTATIONS

These are small and occasional alterations in the DNA nucleotides of a gene, usually with certain bases being replaced by others. As a result, they can cause changes in the mRNA and the protein it codes. They cannot be seen by an optical microscope, as they usually only affect a few nucleotides. Occasionally, if one amino acid is exchanged for another, the protein can continue to carry out its function, but if it cannot, the effects will be observed in the phenotype.

3.1 Genetic disorders

The various alterations that genetic material can experience produce a series of phenotype disorders. These disorders can be due to:

- mutations occurring on a single gene, such as with **haemophilia** and **sickle-cell disease**.
- the combination of certain alleles of various genes, such as with certain types of **cancer**.
- alterations in chromosome number, such as the case of **Down's syndrome**.

The inheritance of genetic disorders depends on the type of cell where the mutations arise.

- **Non-hereditary genetic disorders** are caused by mutations in somatic cells due to exposure to **mutagenic agents**, such as tobacco, ionising radiation and certain chemical substances. These mutations are not usually harmful, unless they affect cancer-related genes.
- **Hereditary genetic disorders** are caused when mutations occur in reproductive cells, which affect all the cells of the offspring. Certain types of cancer, such as pancreatic and **bowel** cancer, are largely hereditary. Down's syndrome affects one in every 1 000 births. It is caused by a fault in gametogenesis whereby the embryo receives three copies of chromosome 21.

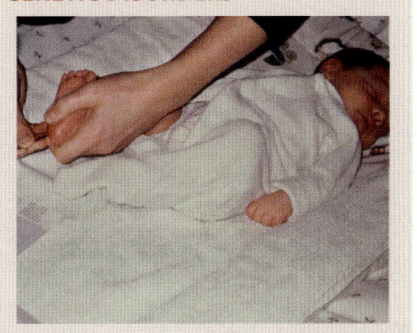

MUTATIONS AND EVOLUTION

The genetic variability that enables the evolution of the species by **natural selection** increases through mutations. As a result, they are considered beneficial in terms of the species' evolution, although they can be harmful for the individual.

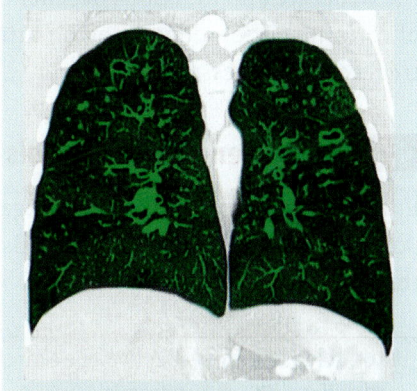

◯ **Cystic fibrosis** is a hereditary genetic disorder that affects the respiratory and digestive systems. People with cystic fibrosis inherit a defective gene on chromosome 7 called *CFTR*.

PREVENTION AND THE SOCIAL IMPACT OF GENETIC DISORDERS

The prevention of genetic disorders is based on genetic screening to verify the existence of the responsible mutation. One of these is the **heel-prick** test, which is performed on newborns.

If a mutation is found, screening is extended to the close family to locate its source and incidence in others. Medical protocols are also put in place for treatment.

ACTIVITIES

15. How are chromosomal mutations classified?

16. Mutations can have negative, positive or no consequences at all for the living organisms in which they occur. Find out more about this and write a short report to help explain this statement.

17. Which seems more serious, nullisomy or monosomy? Explain your answer.

18. Indicate whether the genetic fault causing the following disorders could be detected with an optical microscope.
    a. haemophilia
    b. Down's syndrome
    c. pancreatic cancer
    d. cystic fibrosis

4 Genetic engineering

> What is *in situ* hybridisation used for?

The advances made in molecular genetics since the 1950s have made **genetic engineering** possible now. This comprises the study and techniques of gene manipulation and the transfer of genes from one organism to another.

The use of these methods has made it possible for genes to be exchanged between different species. Genetic engineering aims to increase knowledge of the structure and functions of genetic material and improve the biological traits of certain species, depending on human interests, and prevent, diagnose and treat certain illnesses.

4.1 Genetic engineering tools

Enzymes are used to manipulate genes and cut, stick, synthesise and break down the molecules of nucleic acids. The most commonly used enzymes are the following:

Exonucleases. These join to a nucleic acid and cut it up into individual nucleotides, starting from one end. This is how isolated nucleotides are obtained.

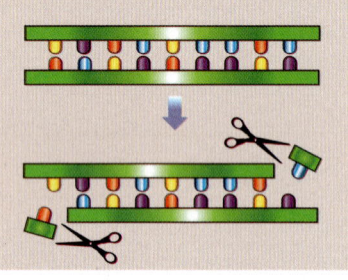

Endonucleases. These cut the nucleic acid at intermediate points in the molecule, producing segments of nucleic acid of varying sizes.

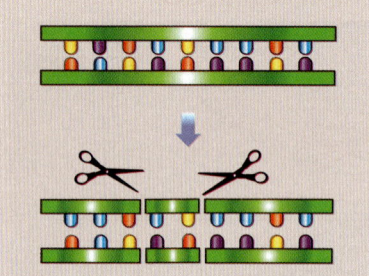

Restriction nucleases or restrictases. These cut the nucleic acid in places with specific base sequences, which are called restriction sites. The cut can produce a straight cut with 'blunt' ends or an overhang with 'sticky' ends.

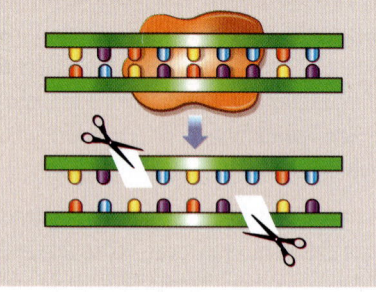

Polymerases. These can be DNA or RNA. They add nucleotides to a strand, provided that there is a template strand.

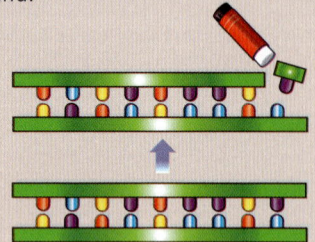

Transferases. These add nucleotides to one end of RNA or DNA in a single strand without the need for a template strand.

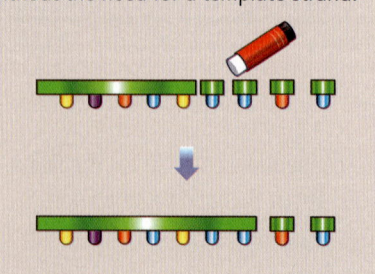

Ligases. These catalyse the union of two strands of DNA, two molecules of RNA or two molecules of single-stranded DNA.

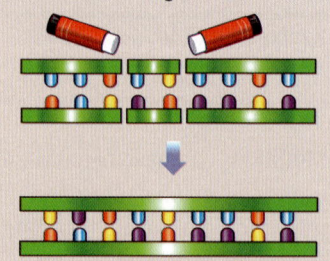

ACTIVITIES

19. The terms *molecular genetics*, *genetic engineering* and *biotechnology* are very closely related and frequently used as synonyms by the media. Do you think this is right? Explain your answer.

4.2 Genetic engineering techniques

Genetic engineering techniques are very varied and are constantly developing. They include the hybridisation of nucleic acids, the creation of transgenic organisms and various types of cloning.

HYBRIDISATION OF NUCLEIC ACIDS

Hybridisation is the process by which two complementary strands of nucleic acid pair up and form a double helix. Knowledge of this process has allowed for the development of a very useful technique called *in situ* **hybridisation**, which can detect specific sequences of nucleotides. It consists of using a single-stranded segment of DNA or mRNA to locate, through hybridisation, genes or other sequences of nucleotides in cells, tissue or chromosomes.

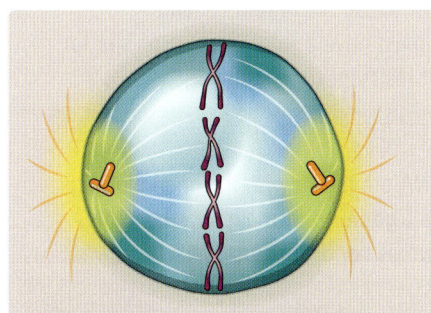

- The cells to examine are prepared in metaphase to be able to easily identify the chromosomes. 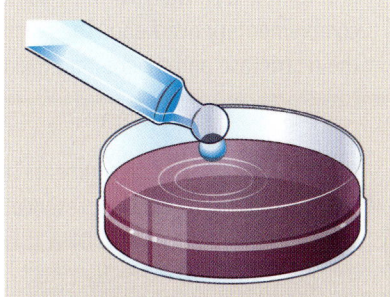
- They are incubated with radioactively-marked mRNA. The mRNA used comprises the coding sequences for the protein whose gene is to be located.
- From photographs, it is possible to detect the areas of the chromosomes that have the greatest radioactivity. 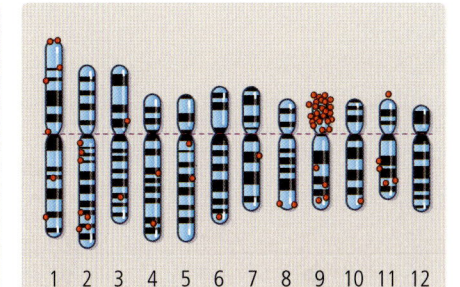

CREATION OF TRANSGENIC ORGANISMS

Transgenic or **genetically modified organisms** (**GMO**) are useful for medical research, cell biology and agriculture. A **transgenic organism** has had a foreign or modified gene inserted into it from another cell or organism and is able to transmit it to its offspring.

TRANSGENIC ANIMALS
In animals, much work has been carried out on mammals, especially mice. Transgenic mice have been created so that their phenotypes imitate aspects of human conditions, such as arteriosclerosis, diabetes, cystic fibrosis, Alzheimer's and many types of cancer. The aim is to develop more effective treatments for these disorders.

TRANSGENIC PLANTS
Transgenic plants are created more easily than transgenic animals. Plants that come with the desired amounts of certain nutrients in their seeds are grown. In the same way, resistance to **pests** and infections and tolerance of environmental conditions in extreme habitats such as marshland have been achieved.

ACTIVITIES

20. Do you think that a segment of a protein could be used directly to locate the gene that codes for it in the DNA by *in situ* hybridisation? Explain your answer.

21. Find out why it is technically easier to create transgenic plants than transgenic animals.

22. Search for information on the use of various transgenic organisms that are currently being sold.

23. Find out about eugenics and euphenics, and write a report on both. Which of the two seems to be more acceptable from an ethical point of view?

DNA CLONING

DNA cloning is a technique that involves inserting a segment of DNA into any species, to make copies of it or to express it in a cell through a cloning vector.

A **cloning vector** is a DNA molecule that is able to replicate and express its genes within a cell. The most commonly used are **plasmids** (small circular DNA molecules found in some bacteria) and **bacteriophages** (viruses that naturally infect bacteria).

CLONING WITH PLASMIDS

1 To **clone** using a **plasmid** as a vector, the DNA to clone and the plasmid are treated separately with the same restrictase to create the same complementary overhang. The plasmid must have a single restriction site for the restrictase and a gene that makes it resistant to an antibiotic.

2 The segments of DNA are mixed with the open plasmids in the presence of a **ligase**, to fit them together. This hybrid DNA is known as **recombinant DNA**.

3 By mixing the plasmids with the bacteria, the recombinant DNA enters one of them; in this way they become antibiotic-resistant bacteria.

4 If the bacteria are cultivated in the presence of the antibiotic, those which have not incorporated the plasmid will be eliminated and those which have done so will survive, as they are resistant. As such, through successive bacteria cultures, it is possible to obtain many copies of a certain gene to use it in other techniques, such as the production of a certain protein that is of interest.

> Currently, the majority of human insulin, used to treat **diabetes**, is created from cloning with plasmids. A plasmid with the human insulin gene is inserted into *Escherichia coli* bacteria, which is cultivated industrially to produce insulin.

ACTIVITIES

24. The term *cloning* is used in genetic engineering, but does it always mean the same thing? Explain your answer.

25. A segment of DNA is to be cloned using a plasmid that has no gene for antibiotic resistance as the cloning vector. Will the cloning work? Why/why not?

26. To insert a DNA segment into a plasmid, it is necessary to cut and stick the DNA molecules. Which enzymes are essential for this to happen?

27. Search for information on Dolly the sheep and her importance in science.

REPRODUCTIVE CLONING

Reproductive cloning consists of obtaining an individual that is genetically identical to the original. To do this, the nucleus of an ovule is replaced by the nucleus of a somatic cell of another organism of the same species. The modified ovule is then implanted into the uterus of a female of the same species, in which it develops to create a cloned individual. This individual is genetically identical to the donor of the nucleus.

This technique has been used to clone sheep, pigs and mice. Its interest, for the moment, lies in the knowledge generated by its research.

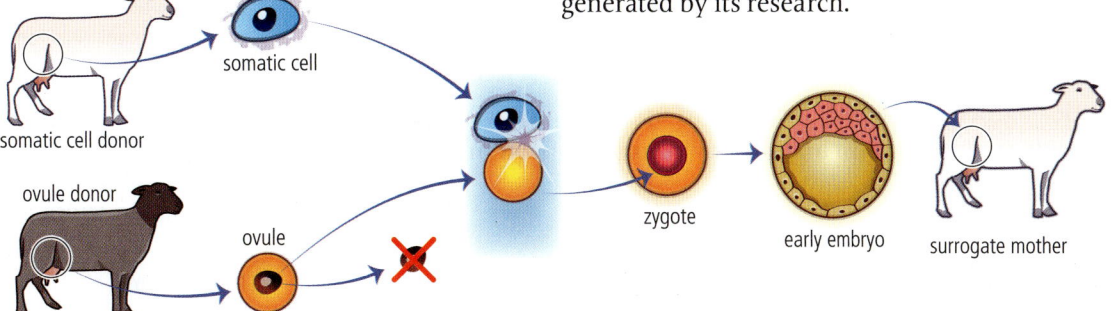

THERAPEUTIC CLONING

Therapeutic cloning is the use of **embryonic stem cells** to regenerate tissues in the treatment of conditions caused by the abnormal functioning or poor state of a certain type of cell. This type of cell therapy avoids the need for organ transplants, although rejection by the patient's immune system can still occur. To avoid this from happening, the nucleus of the embryonic stem cell is replaced by a cell nucleus of the person affected by the condition, in the same way that an animal is cloned. The tissue then regenerates, with the same genetic information as the patient, and is not immunologically rejected.

Stem cells are cells which can be constantly renewed through cell division to become any type of specialised adult cell in a specific tissue. One specific type of stem cell is known as an **embryonic stem cell**.

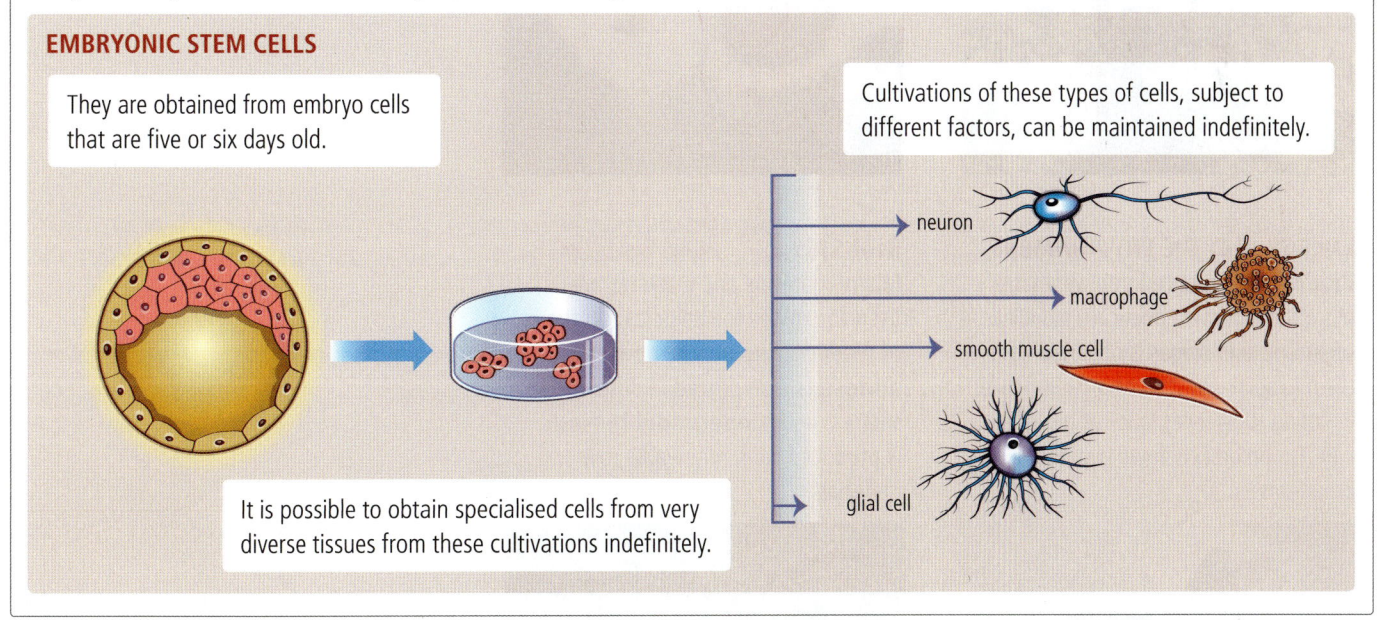

EMBRYONIC STEM CELLS

They are obtained from embryo cells that are five or six days old.

Cultivations of these types of cells, subject to different factors, can be maintained indefinitely.

It is possible to obtain specialised cells from very diverse tissues from these cultivations indefinitely.

ACTIVITIES

28. In therapeutic cloning, what is the reason for replacing the nucleus of the embryonic stem cell with a cell nucleus from the patient?

29. List the advantages of embryonic stem cells compared with stem cells from other tissues.

5. Biotechnology and bioethics

> What is the controversy over biotechnology?

Biotechnology comprises the knowledge and techniques that enable biological systems (such as live organisms, cells, organelles and enzymes) to be used and practically exploited in the production of goods and services.

This definition covers age-old activities, including the production of alcoholic **beverages** like wine and beer, fermented bread and cheese and other products fermented from milk. Biotechnology's current relevance is linked to the use of genetic engineering, which has opened up its application in different areas of agriculture, food, health and the environment. Below are some such examples.

> **BIOTECHNOLOGICAL PROCESS PARTS**
>
> **Biocatalysts** are unicellular or multicellular organisms, cultivations of animal or plant cells, and even isolated enzymes used to obtain a certain product.
>
> **Bioreactors** are tanks (usually made of stainless steel) in which different reactions are carried out to convert a specific substrate into a product, aided by biocatalysts.

LIVESTOCK AND AGRICULTURE
Genetically modified plants and animals are created with greater productivity and resistance to diseases than organisms found in nature. Vaccines, fertilisers and insecticides are also created, and products, such as milk rich in hormones or **clotting factors**, are obtained for their use in drugs.

FOOD AND HEALTH
Nutrient-enriched or special food for diabetics and allergy-sufferers is created from genetically modified organisms. Vaccines, antibiotics, hormones and other substances are also produced from modified microorganisms and used as drugs.

ENERGY AND THE ENVIRONMENT
Biodiesel is produced from vegetable oils obtained from genetically modified organisms and biogas is obtained from the microbial digestion of organic waste. Polluting substances (such as oil spills) can also be broken down by using microorganisms.

INDUSTRY
Microorganisms and enzymes are used to replace the chemical synthesis of products, the treatment of **raw materials** is improved in different sectors, and **biodegradable** plastic is produced from renewable raw materials.

> **ACTIVITIES**
>
> 30. Research some of the most well-known biotechnological processes of ancient civilisations.

Ethical implications of biotechnology

The current biotechnological revolution and its economic, social and ecological impacts have raised controversial ethical questions. Society, as the main beneficiary of scientific and technological innovations, must decide whether these innovations are ethically desirable.

Bioethics is the set of moral principles that govern human action on the evolution and spontaneous development of living organisms.

SOME ETHICALLY CONTROVERSIAL BIOTECHNOLOGICAL ADVANCES

TRANSGENIC FOOD
Transgenic food began to be sold in the last decade of the 20th century. Since then, its use has been controversial because of its potential health and environmental risks.

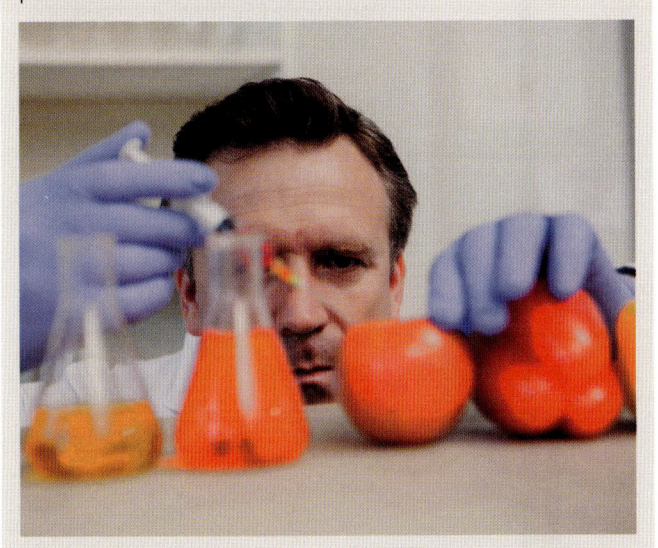

FREEZING OF HUMAN EMBRYOS
The freezing of human embryos and their subsequent **thawing** for implantation in the mother's uterus has also created controversy, especially in relation to the potential use of leftover embryos.

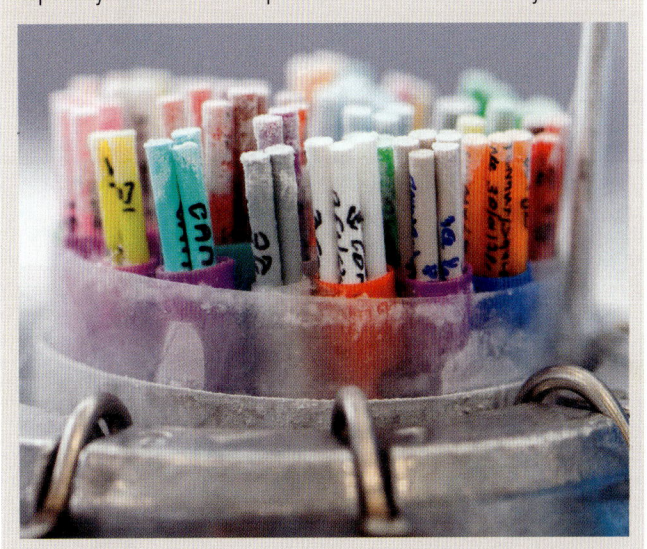

ASSISTED REPRODUCTION AND ANTENATAL DIAGNOSIS
Antenatal diagnosis detects hereditary disorders in the foetus. Artificial insemination and in-vitro fertilisation spark a debate when they involve resorting to **surrogate mothers** or when the diagnosis means the selection of healthy embryos.

STEM CELLS AND THERAPEUTIC CLONING
The use of stem cells obtained from human embryos, for their use in cell therapy without the risk of immunological rejection continues to fuel debates. Obtaining pluripotent stem cells from skin is the beginning of the resolution of the moral dilemma of using embryonic stem cells.

ACTIVITIES

31. What is your opinion of using surrogate mothers? Tell your classmates what you think and participate in a discussion on the subject.

32. What is the difference between antenatal diagnosis and pre-implantation diagnosis?

33. Since genetically modified organisms began to be sold at the end of the last century, great controversy has surrounded the subject. Search for information in different resources on the main arguments for and against GMOs and share your findings with your classmates. Present the different arguments and the conclusions you reach on posters.

Discovery techniques

LEARN ABOUT THE POLYMERASE CHAIN REACTION

> What are the steps in the polymerase chain reaction?

The **polymerase chain reaction**, or **PCR**, is a technique that allows many copies of double-stranded DNA molecules to be made *in vitro* without having to clone them in bacteria. The steps to follow for this technique are as follows:

1. The ends of the DNA must be of a known sequence so that known segments can be added on.

2. Subsequently, the DNA is heated to separate its two strands. Then, short segments of DNA of a sequence complementary to the ends are added so that, once the mixture has cooled, they match up. These two short segments, known as **primers**, will be used by the polymerase to add nucleotides, as without their participation, the enzyme would not work.

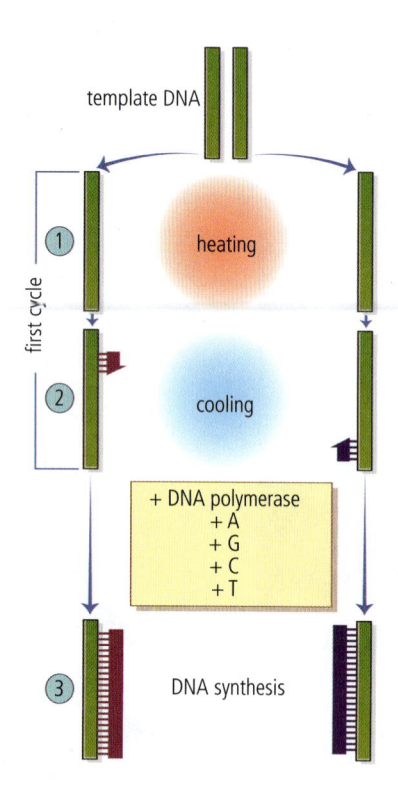

APPLICATIONS OF THE POLYMERASE CHAIN REACTION

DNA cloning in bacteria takes several days, while PCR clones it in hours. It is used to quickly diagnose genetic disorders and to detect low levels of viral infections, given that it is a very sensitive technique. PCR also enables samples as small as a single cell to be analysed, which is very useful in forensic medicine.

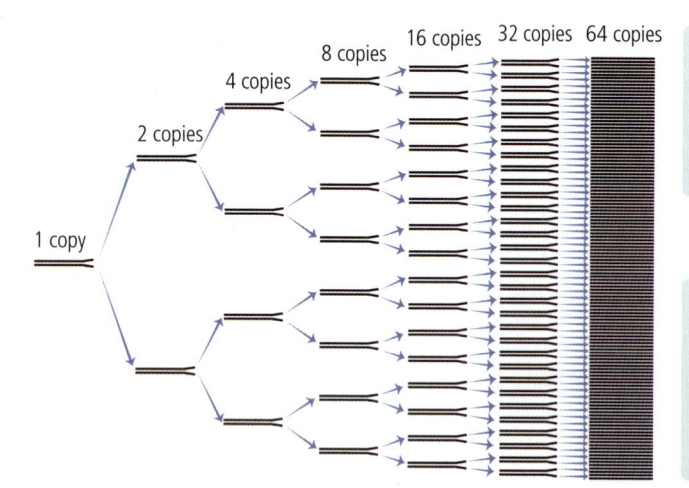

3. The polymerase and the four nucleotides with the corresponding bases (A, G, T and C) are added. In this way, the template chains are synthesised, and the first replication cycle is completed.

4. The cycle is repeated over and again so that the DNA is copied exponentially, as the DNA molecules synthesised in a cycle are used as templates for the following cycle. After 30 cycles, the right amount of DNA can be obtained.

ACTIVITIES

1. In your own words, explain the steps involved in the polymerase chain reaction. What are the advantages of this technique?

Discovery techniques

SOLVING MOLECULAR GENETICS PROBLEMS

> How can we determine the polypeptide corresponding to a DNA strand?

Determining the polypeptide corresponding to a DNA strand

To resolve problems on the processes of replication, transcription and translation, use the genetic code table to find out which amino acid corresponds to each codon.

Follow the steps that appear below to determine the polypeptide corresponding to the following DNA strand, if the coding strand is the one at the top:

ATGTTTGGTAATTGTGGG
TACAAACCATTAACACCC

1. Write the two strands separately and label them as strands of the original molecule. Write the bases that correspond to the new complementary strand below the top strand and above the bottom strand. Label the newly synthesised strands.

ATGTTTGGTAATTGTGGGTAA
TACAAACCATTAACACCCATT

→

ATGTTTGGTAATTGTGGGTAA — original molecule strand
TACAAACCATTAACACCCATT
ATGTTTGGTAATTGTGGGTAA
TACAAACCATTAACACCCATT — original molecule strand

newly synthesised strands

2. As the coding strand is the top one, take the bottom one as a template and write the sequence of RNA bases, changing T for U.

ATGTTTGGTAATTGTGGGTAA
TACAAACCATTAACACCCATT

→

ATGTTTGGTAATTGTGGGTAA
AUGUUUGGUAAUUGUGGGUAA — mRNA strand
TACAAACCATTAACACCCATT

3. Search in the genetic code table for the amino acids corresponding to each codon.

AUG-UUU-GGU-AAU-UGU-GGG-UAA

methionine-phenylalanine-glycine-asparagine-cysteine-glycine-stop

ACTIVITIES

1. State the polypeptide corresponding to each DNA strand.
   ATGATAACTTTGCCCGTGTAA
   TACTATTGAAACGGGCACATT

2. Explain what the DNA codons TAA and ATT represent.

3. Who invented and developed the polymerase chain reaction technique? Look for information on Internet and write a short report about this topic.

UNIT 04 Molecular genetics

Revision activities

1 Indicate which of the following statements are incorrect and explain why.

  a. In 1944, and building on bacterial transformation experiments, the Canadian Frederick Griffith and his collaborators demonstrated that deoxyribonucleic acid (DNA) was a hereditary substance.

  b. At the end of the 19th century, the Swiss scientist Friedrich Miescher (1844–1895) isolated, in the cell nuclei of salmon spermatozoa, an acid substance rich in phosphorus, which he called nuclein. It was thus proven that nucleic acid is a hereditary substance.

  c. In 1953, James Watson and Francis Crick, building on the research of Rosalind Franklin and Raymond Gosling, proposed a three-dimensional model for the DNA molecule.

2 Frederick Griffith and Oswald T. Avery were two researchers who carried out experiments in which they proved that DNA is an inherited substance. Prepare a presentation in which you explain how their experiments worked and how they managed to demonstrate the function of DNA.

3 Read the following text and develop a hypothesis explaining why phenylketonuria is hereditary.

  "Phenylketonuria is a hereditary metabolic disorder that comprises the accumulation of phenylpyruvate in the blood, a toxic substance which causes severe mental retardation. This accumulation is due to the absence of an enzyme present in the healthy population, which catalyses the reaction converting the amino acid phenylalanine into another, known as tyrosine. This reaction prevents the excessive formation of the toxic substance."

4 What molecular process is represented in the following diagram? Copy it into your notebook and write down its steps.

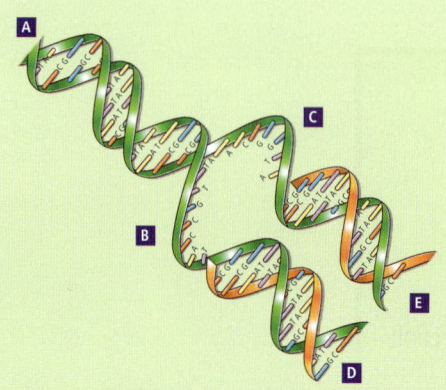

5 Explain the following statement:

  DNA replication is a semi-conservative process.

6 State the base sequence of the two segments resulting from the replication of the following double-stranded segment of DNA:

  AGCGGTGTGAGCACGCTC
  TCGCCACACTCGTGCGAG

7 State the sequence of complementary bases for each of the following DNA strands:

  a. TATGAATAGGCACTGTT
  b. TTGCAGGTAACCGTAAT
  c. AAGCGCCGTATAATTCGC
  d. GCGCATTAGGCATGCGGG

8 Compare DNA with RNA in terms of their structure and functions.

9 Look at the following sequences and select those that are DNA. If they relate to the coding strands, transcribe them as RNA:

  a. AUGAGCAGCUUAUUGUC
  b. TTATTAAACGCGTCGCGA
  c. CCAGCCGCAAAGCCGGCCG
  d. GTCTCGGATACTCGAGCCC
  e. TCGTCGGAGTCCTCGGTCA
  f. GGGUCUCUCUGGAGUCACA

10 What happens when a messenger RNA is translating in the ribosome and the triplet UUU appears? What about when UUC appears? What is the reason for this coincidence?

11 Write down the mRNA base sequences that would be transcribed from the following DNA molecules. Remember that the coding strand is the bottom strand.

  a. ATTGCCAATTGGCCTA
     TAACGGTTAACCGGAT
  b. GGGGCTTAACGCAATC
     CCCCGAATTGCGTTAG
  c. TGGGATATAGCGCGCC
     ACCCTATATCGCGCGG

12 What is a nucleotide? Are all nucleotides the same? Explain your answers.

13 Name the nucleotides that DNA is made of and indicate which nitrogenous bases pair up.

14 Briefly describe the process shown in the following image.

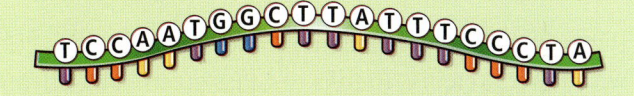

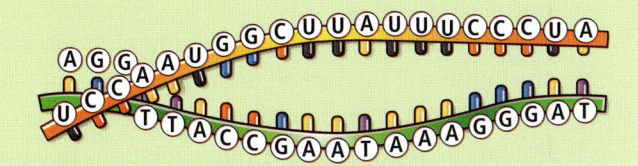

15 A segment of a protein has the following sequence of amino acids:

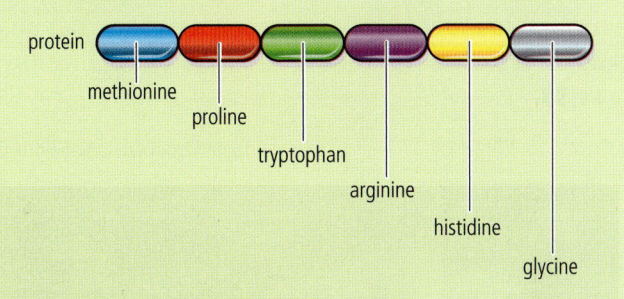

protein
methionine
proline
tryptophan
arginine
histidine
glycine

Find out the sequence of the mRNA bases which it has been translated from, from right to left, and answer the questions.

a. What would happen if, in the codon for tryptophan, a mutation changed the G on the right to an A?
b. What would happen if the A on the codon for histidine was replaced by a G because of a mutation on the DNA from which it had been transcribed?
c. Which of the three bases of the codon for glycine can mutate so that, upon translation of the mRNA, glycine continues to be positioned in the protein?

16 Explain whether the following statement is true or false:

RNA transcribes DNA so that, subsequently, it can be translated in ribosomes to produce a polypeptide.

17 Search for journalistic articles on food additives and the possibility of mutagenesis. Write a short report with the information that you find and present it in class. Discuss this subject with your classmates.

18 Is there a link between the terms *plasmid* and *bacteriophage*? Explain your answer.

19 Is a transgenic organism the same as a cloned organism? Explain your answer.

20 Relate each of the following enzymes to its function: exonuclease, endonuclease, restrictase, polymerase, transferase, ligase.

a. It can be DNA or RNA. They add nucleotides to a strand, provided that another strand serves as a template.
b. It adds nucleotides to the end of a single strand of DNA or RNA without the need for a template.
c. It catalyses the union of two strands of DNA, two molecules of RNA or two single-stranded molecules of DNA.
d. It joins to a nucleic acid and cuts it up into nucleotides, starting from one end.
e. It cuts the nucleic acid at intermediate points in the molecule, producing segments of nucleic acid of varying sizes.
f. It cuts the nucleic acid in places with specific base sequences, which are called restriction sites. The cut can produce a straight cut with 'blunt' ends or an overhang with 'sticky' ends.

21 Look for information on transgenic organisms and clones. Then, write a brief report on the subject.

22 In genetic engineering, the plasmid pBR322 is used as a cloning vector. It carries two genes for resistance to the antibiotics ampicillin and tetracycline. On both genes, there are restriction sites for the restrictases on which foreign DNA can be inserted. What is the advantage of using this plasmid as a cloning vector, compared with others which have only one antibiotic-resistant gene?

23 Read the following text and write a statement that summarises its contents:

"Since its creation in 1993, the mission of the International Bioethics Committee of UNESCO (United Nations Educational, Scientific and Cultural Organization) has been to ensure that advances in biotechnology and genetic engineering do not infringe upon the principles of freedom and human dignity. In October 2005, the UNESCO General Conference approved the Universal Declaration on Bioethics and Human Rights addressed to States and which deals with ethical matters related to medicine, life sciences and technologies applied to humans, taking into consideration their social, legal and environmental dimensions."

Read and think

HOW THE JELLYFISH'S GREEN LIGHT REVOLUTIONISED BIOSCIENCE

"In the 1960s, when the Japanese scientist Osamu Shimomura began to study the bioluminescent jellyfish *Aequorea victoria*, he had no idea what a scientific revolution it would lead to.

When scientists develop methods to help them see things that were once invisible, research always takes a great leap forward.

The 2008 Nobel Prize in Chemistry, awarded to Osamu Shimomura, Martin Chalfie, and Roger Y. Tsien, rewarded a similar effect on science. The green fluorescent protein, GFP, has functioned in the past few decades as a guiding star for biochemists, biologists, medical scientists and other researchers. The strong green colour of this protein appears under blue and ultraviolet light. It can, for example, illuminate growing cancer tumours or show the development of Alzheimer's disease in the brain or the growth of pathogenic bacteria. What was revolutionary about GFP is that the protein does not need any additives to glow, in contrast to other bioluminescent proteins, which require a continuous supply of energy-rich molecules.

An even more interesting use of GFP means that researchers can actually follow processes inside individual cells. The more researchers know about a cell type – how it develops and functions – the greater the chance that they can develop effective treatments with minimal side effects.

The chemical processes of cells are usually regulated by proteins. There are tens of thousands of different proteins, each with different functions. By connecting GFP to one of these proteins, researchers can obtain vital information. They can see which cells a particular protein inhabits, and they can follow its movements and watch its interactions with other proteins. Thanks to GFP's green light, scientists can now track a single protein under the microscope.

When Osamu Shimomura began to study biofluorescent organisms in the sea, he wanted to understand what made them shine. This is a typical example of how basic research can lead to an unexpected scientific revolution. However, one mystery remains to be solved. Why does the jellyfish *Aequorea victoria* shine? Many organisms living in the sea use light from biofluorescent proteins to confuse their enemies, to attract food or to tempt a partner. But no one knows yet what has caused *Aequorea victoria* to display GFP."

Adapted from www.nobelprize.com

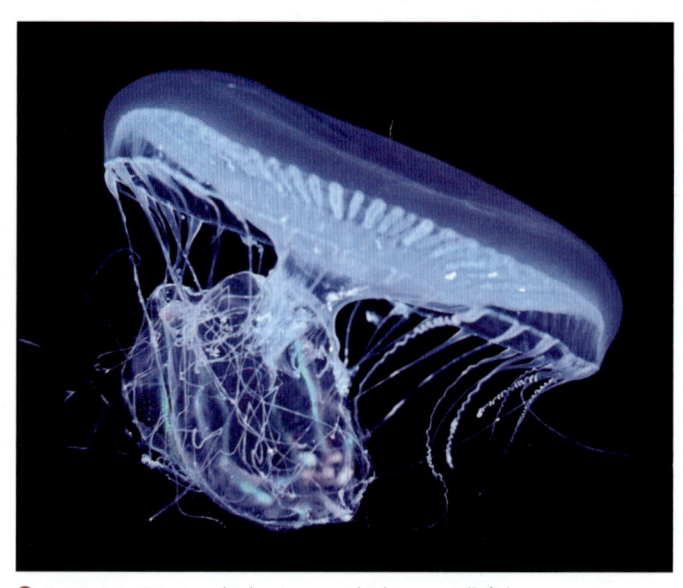

Aequorea victoria, a bioluminescent hydrozoan jellyfish

ANSWER THE QUESTIONS

1. What is GFP? How was it discovered?
2. Why is the discovery of GFP considered to be so important in the field of molecular genetics?
3. What makes GFP better than other fluorescent proteins previously used in research?
4. Find some medical applications of GFP research in the text.
5. Can the use of GFP in research be considered an example of genetic engineering? Why or why not?
6. Using GFP in research implies genetically modifying organisms. However, this can lead to a better understanding of disease and even to the discovery of new treatments. Hold an in class-debate about some of the ethical implications of these processes.

Work it out

CONCEPT MAP

Use the words in the word cloud to create your own unit map in your notebook. Write any connecting texts you need.

ADN
ARN
nucleic acids
transcription
chromosome mutation
replication
in situ hybridisation
gene mutation
Molecular genetics
therapeutic cloning
mutations
reproductive cloning
DNA cloning
genetic engineering
creation of transgenic organisms

SELF-ASSESSMENT

Carry out a self-assessment of what you learned in this unit. Choose one answer for each question and then check your answers.

1 Which of the following is different between RNA and DNA?
   a. The number of nucleotide strands
   b. The cytoplasmic location
   c. The presence of adenine

2 What do DNA polymerases do during DNA replication?
   a. Separate DNA strands so they can act as templates.
   b. Add complementary nucleotides to the strand being replicated.
   c. Release enzymes from DNA after replication has been completed.

3 Anticodons are found in ...
   a. DNA
   b. mRNA
   c. tRNA

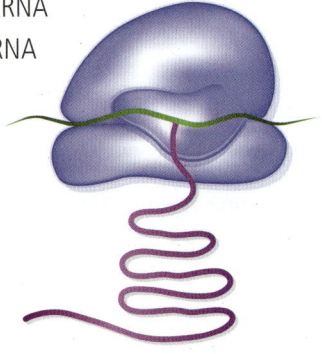

4 Which of the following is not a chromosome mutation?
   a. DNA translocation
   b. Polyploidy
   c. Replacement of a few DNA bases

5 Which of the following does not help to prevent the development of genetic disorders?
   a. Trait hybridisation
   b. Genetic testing of newborns
   c. Avoidance of mutagenic substances

6 Which cut nucleic acids at intermediate points in the molecule?
   a. ligases
   b. transferases
   c. endonucleases

7 Which of these is not used in DNA cloning?
   a. Viruses
   b. Plasmids
   c. Fungi

8 Which of these statements about embryonic stem cells is false?
   a. They can be grown indefinitely.
   b. They come from 20-day-old embryo cells.
   c. They can be cultured into specialised tissues.

9 Which of these liquids is not produced using biotechnology?
   a. Biodiesel
   b. Milk
   c. Beer

10 The set of moral principles that govern human action on the evolution and spontaneous development of living organisms is called ...
   a. Biotechnology.
   b. Bioengineering.
   c. Bioethics.

Glossary

A

alleviate (v): to make something less intense or more bearable

antibody (n): a protein produced by the body's immune system that detects and destroys invaders (antigens) such as bacteria and viruses

antigen (n): a substance, such as toxins, viruses and bacteria, that when introduced into the body stimulates the production of an antibody

assortment (n): separation into classes, distribution, classification

attach (v): to join to something

average (n): a number calculated by adding several amounts together, finding a total and dividing the total by the number of amounts

B

be ahead of someone's time (exp): having ideas or attitudes that are too advanced to be acceptable in the present time

be awarded (exp): to get a reward or prize

bear in mind (exp): to remember to consider something when you are making decisions or thinking about a matter

become engrossed with something (exp): occupy someone's mind or attention completely with something

beverage (n): a liquid for drinking, usually excluding water.

biodegradable (adj): easily decomposed by natural agents like water, oxygen, ultraviolet rays, microorganisms, etc.

biodiesel (n): a clean renewable fuel made using natural vegetable oils and fats

bowel (n): the long tube in the body that helps digest food and carries solid waste out of the body

breakage (n): damage or loss as a result of breaking

C

cell culture (n): maintenance and growth of cells in a medium and under precise conditions after having been removed from the body

churn out (ph v): to produce something in large quantities

clotting factor (n): substance in the blood that is involved in its coagulation

colony (n): several individual organisms of the same species living together in close association

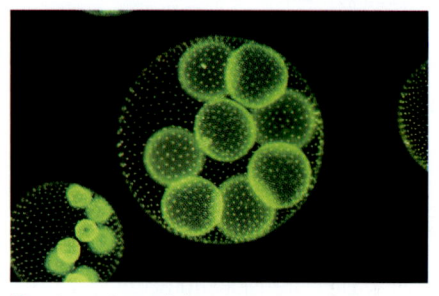

⬤ Colony of unicellular algae

concerning (prep): relating to

cross-pollinating (n): the transfer of pollen from the flower of one plant to the flower of another plant

cyanobacteria (n): (singular cyanobacterium) a group of photosynthetic, nitrogen fixing bacteria often called blue-green algae, that can be found in almost every terrestrial and aquatic habitat

⬤ Colony of photosynthetic cyanobacteria (genus *Nostoc*)

D

diabetes (n): a condition where the amount of glucose in the blood is too high because the body cannot use it properly

diffraction (n): the bending of waves around obstacles in their path

diffusion (n): the movement of particles (atoms, ions or molecules) from a region in which they are in higher concentration to regions of lower concentration

distilled water (n): water that has had many of its impurities, such as dissolved salts, removed through distillation

dogma (n): a theory or belief that is formally defined, stated, and thought to be true

drawback (n): a disadvantage or inconvenience

dropper (n): a small tube with a rubber container at one end that is used to measure out liquids by drops

⬤ Dropper

dye (n): a substance used to change the colour of something

E

encase (v): to surround or cover something or someone completely

endothermic reaction (n): a process or reaction that absorbs energy in the form of heat

enzyme (n): a protein produced by cells which help in chemical reactions

exothermic reaction (n): a reaction or process that release energy, usually in the form of heat or light.

🔺 Combustion is an exothermic reaction.

eyepiece (n): the lens or group of lenses closest to the eye in an optical instrument such a microscope

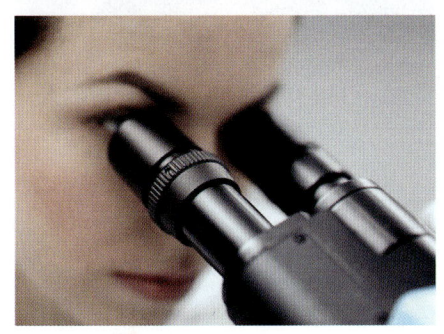

🔺 Eyepiece of a microscope

F

framework (n): a skeletal structure designed to support or enclose something

G

glaucoma (n): an eye condition in which the fluid pressure inside the eye rises to a level higher than healthy and which, eventually, may damage the optic nerve, causing the loss of vision

growth medium (n): (also called *culture medium*) a sterilised solution that contains the substances required for the growth of microorganisms such as bacteria, protozoans, fungi, etc.

guinea pig (n): small rodent of the genus *Cavia* widely kept as a pet and used in biomedical research

🔺 Domestic guinea pig (*Cavia porcellus*)

H

heel-prick test (n): a screening test to detect genetic disorders based on measuring the concentrations of amino acids in a small sample of blood taken by pricking the heel of the newborn baby

honeycomb (n): a structure of hexagonal, thin-walled cells made by honeybees to hold honey and larvae

humble (adj): modest or low in rank

hurdle (n): a problem or difficulty

L

linked (adj): associated

M

magnification power (n): a measure of the ability of a lens or other optical instruments to enlarge the image of an object, expressed as the ratio of the size of the image to that of the object

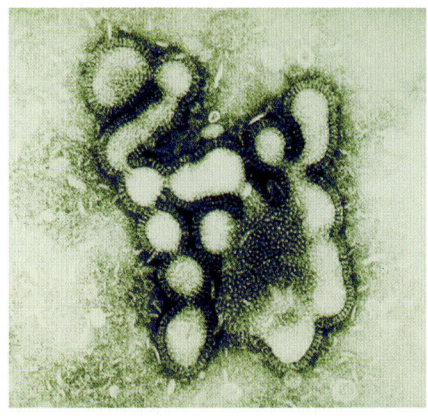

🔺 Influenza virus at 295 000 magnification

manipulation (n): modification or alteration

meshlike (adj): made of material like a net with spaces in it

micrograph (n): a photograph or digital image taken through a microscope to show a magnified image of an object

monocotyledonous plants (n): group of flowering plants, such as grasses, lilies, and palms, having a single cotyledon in the seed, leaves with parallel veins and flower parts in multiples of three

🔺 White lily

N

nail varnish (n): a cosmetic that is applied to the nails to colour them or make them shiny

Glossary

neuron (n): a nerve cell that builds the nervous system and receives and sends electrical signals over long distances within the body

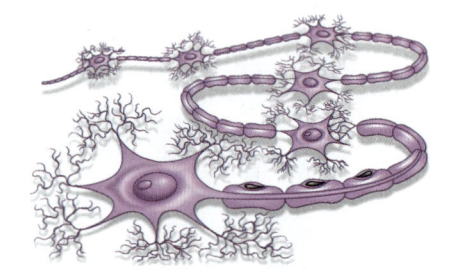

◆ Neuron

neuroscientist (n): a scientist who studies the brain and the nervous system

O

objective (n): the lens nearest to the object being examined in a microscope or other optical instrument

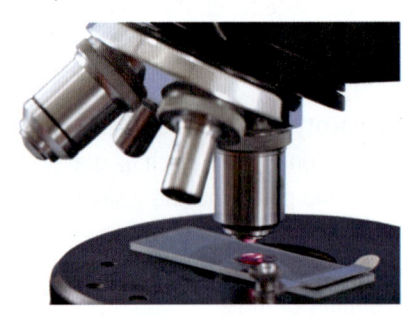

◆ Microscope objective

onset (n): the beginning or start of something

orthopteran insect (n): order of insects that includes grasshoppers, locusts and crickets

◆ Grasshopper

osmosis (n): the diffusion of a fluid, usually water, to pass through a semipermeable membrane from a solution with a low concentration to a solution with a higher concentration until there is an equal concentration on both sides of the membrane

outcome (n): PROBABILITY a possible result of an experiment

P

pest (n): a destructive animal that damages crops or harms livestock

phagocytosis (n): the engulfing of microorganisms or other cells and foreign particles by phagocytes

PhD (n): academic degree conferring the rank and title of doctor awarded by universities in many countries

pinch (v): to squeeze, compress or grip something

pod (n): fruit of a leguminous plant such as pea plants that splits along two sides

◆ Peas in pod

polypeptide (n): a long and continuos chain of amino acids

polysaccharides (n): complex carbohydrates, such as starch and glycogen, composed of 10 to up to several thousand monosaccharides arranged in chains

◆ Starch is a polysaccharide found in potatoes.

potential (adj): possible but not yet achieved

prod (v): to encourage someone to action, to incite

pursue (v): to chase something

R

randomly (adv): happening by chance rather than according to a plan

raw material (n): basic substance in its natural state

regardless of (exp): in spite of

restore (v): to bring back to a state of health

rod-shaped (adj): shaped like a rod, long and cylindrical

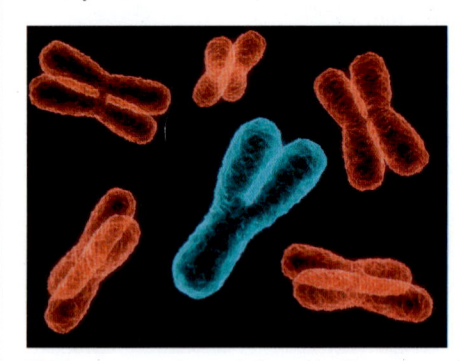

◆ Chromosomes are rod-shaped bodies.

S

self-fertilising (n): the fusion of male and female gametes produced by the same individual

self-pollination (n): the transfer of pollen from the anther to the stigma of the same flower

◆ Pea flowers naturally self-pollinate.

sickle-cell disease (n): a genetic blood disease due to the presence of an abnormal form of hemoglobin, called hemoglobin S, caused by an error in a gene

spindle-shaped (adj): having a shape like a spindle, more or less round in the middle with two ends that are pointed

stain (v): to change colour or dye

strand (n): a thin thread of something

stunt (v): to prevent or impede the growth or development

subscript (n): a number, letter or symbol that is smaller than their normal line of type and is set slightly below

subsequently (adv): occurring or coming later

suitably (adv): in an appropriate manner

surrogate mother (n): woman who agrees to carry someone else's baby and becomes pregnant using some form of assisted reproductive technology

swap (v): to exchange

T

tangle up (ph v): to mix together in a confused mass

template (n): a pattern or mould used to make copies of something

thaw (n): to change from a frozen solid to a liquid because of an increase in temperature

thermal springs (n): a natural spring of water at a temperature higher than the mean temperature of groundwater in the area

◯ Thermal Reserve, New Zealand

turgidity (n): the state of being turgid or swollen, especially due to high water content in plant cells

U

uncoil (v): to make something that is curled or coiled straight

W

workhorses (n): someone or something that works tirelessly

wrap (v): to fold or roll up

◯ Chromosomes are made up of DNA wrapped around proteins.

Big thinkers

Name: Robert Brown
Lived: 1773–1858
Nationality: Scottish
Interests: botany, paleobotany
Bright ideas: He abandoned a career in medicine to study botany. He identified numerous plant families and catalogued thousands of Australian species till then unknown to the mainstream scientific community. He was the first person to name the nucleus in plant cells, and to observe the process which we now call 'Brownian motion'. Both achievements were in part due to his pioneering use of microscope technology, which is now fundamental in laboratory science.

Name: Rosalind Franklin
Lived: 1920–1958
Nationality: English
Interests: chemistry, languages, cricket, hockey
Bright ideas: During her lifetime she was appreciated for studies on coal and graphite, and for leading pioneering work on the structure of viruses, but posthumously, she is remembered as the first person to hypothesise the double-helix DNA molecule. She showed it existed through X-ray diffraction, and her contributions eventually resulted in Nobel Prizes for other people involved. Sadly, she died very young, possibly because of exposure to mutagenic X-ray radiation in her work.

Name: Gregor Mendel
Lived: 1822–1884
Nationality: Austrian
Interests: biological inheritance, scientific method, Christianity
Bright ideas: He is known as the 'father of modern genetics'. He went to the University of Vienna to study botany, zoology, history, maths and physics, but left to become a monk. Mendel applied an experimental approach over fifteen years to establish rules of inheritance (nowadays known as 'Mendel's laws'), even though the mechanism behind his discoveries wasn't discovered until seventy years after his death.

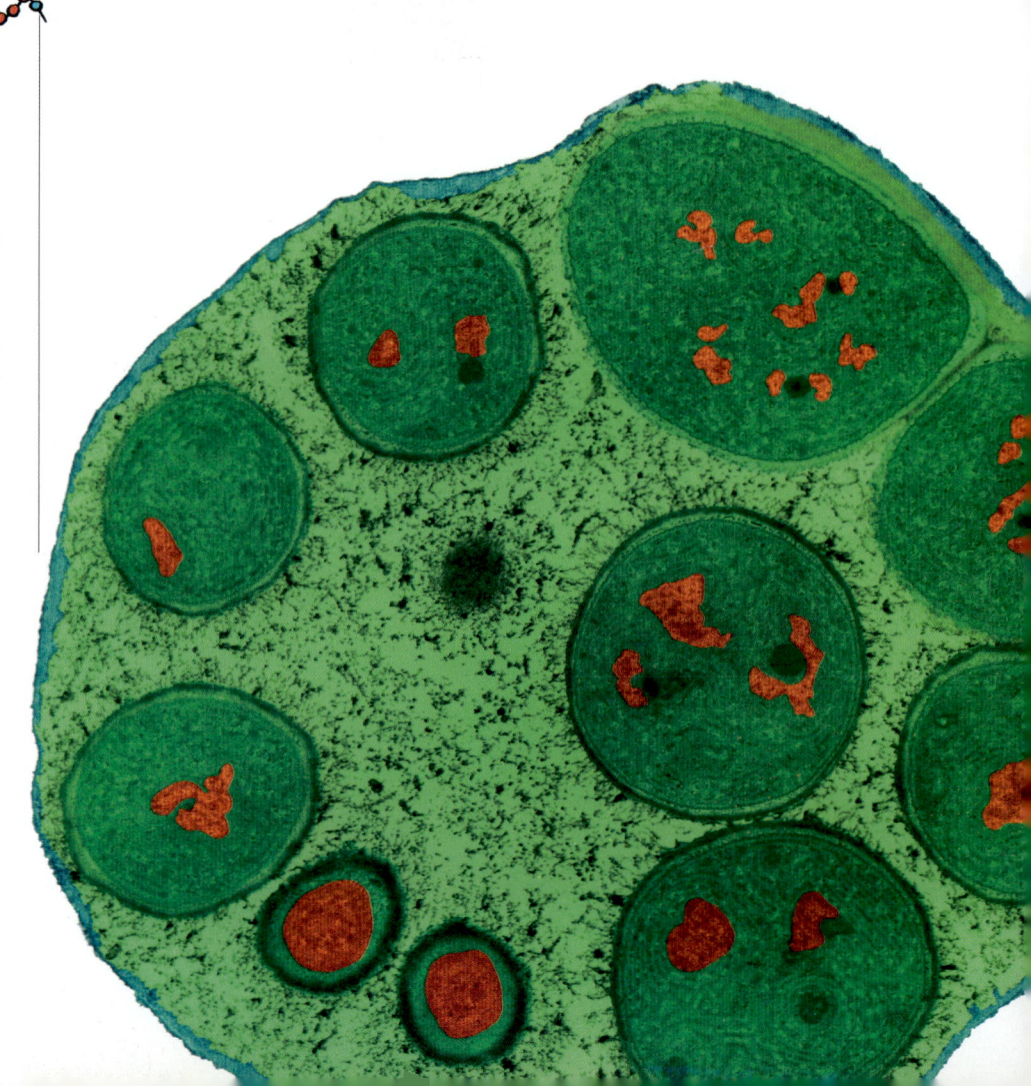

Name: Barbara McClintock
Lived: 1902–1992
Nationality: American
Interests: genetics, swimming, skating, volleyball, tennis
Bright ideas: She was the most distinguished cytogeneticist in history, a researcher at Cornell University considered responsible for more than half her department's important discoveries between 1929 and 1935. Much of her work focused on the reproduction of crop plants, like maize, and in the 1940s and 50s, she identified 'jumping genes', mobile genetic elements. In 1983, she became the only woman to receive an unshared Nobel Prize for Physiology or Medicine.